William Gragg

A cruise in the U.S. steam frigate Mississippi, Wm. C. Nicholson, captain, to China and Japan, from July, 1857, to February, 1860

William Gragg

A cruise in the U.S. steam frigate Mississippi, Wm. C. Nicholson, captain, to China and Japan, from July, 1857, to February, 1860

ISBN/EAN: 9783337184780

Printed in Europe, USA, Canada, Australia, Japan

Cover: Foto ©Andreas Hilbeck / pixelio.de

More available books at **www.hansebooks.com**

A CRUISE

IN THE

U. S. Steam Frigate Mississippi,

WM. C. NICHOLSON, CAPTAIN,

TO

CHINA AND JAPAN

FROM JULY, 1857, TO FEBRUARY, 1860.

BY WILLIAM F. GRAGG.

BOSTON:

DAMRELL & MOORE, PRINTERS,

16 DEVONSHIRE STREET.

1860.

PREFATORY NOTE.

IN presenting this work to my late shipmates and the public, I have confined myself to such matters as have been connected with the cruise; and, in so doing, my aim has been to give a correct statement of affairs, and as full a description of the various places the ship has visited during the cruise as my limited means have permitted. I hope it will prove acceptable to all who may peruse it; and, if it receives their approval, I shall feel satisfied that I have accomplished my point.

CRUISE OF THE MISSISSIPPI.

THE " Mississippi " was put into commission, at the Brooklyn Navy Yard, by Capt. WILLIAM C. NICHOLSON, on the 14th of July, 1857. The following officers reported for duty on board of her: R. N. Stemb'e, I. P. Decatur, Thomas Pattison, Henry Esben, and John G. Sprorton, *Lieutenants;* Thomas B. Nalle, *Purser;* John L. Fox, *Surgeon;* G. W. Bacon, *Master;* Jacob Reed, *Marine Officer;* D. B. Phillips, *Passed Assistant Surgeon;* P. S. Wales, *Assistant Surgeon;* Robert Danby, *Chief Engineer;* T. A. Jackson, Virginius Freeman, *First Assistant Engineers;* Lloyd A. Williams, R. M. Bartleman, *Second Assistant Engineers;* B. C. Bampton, W. P. Desannor, and J. H. Warrington, *Third Assistant Engineers;* James Pritchett, T. B. Mills, J. W. Kelley, Byron Wilson, and Arthur W. Yates, *Midshipmen;* John Bates, *Boatswain;* William Berneice, *Gunner;* Ebenezer Thompson, *Carpenter;* Joseph Bradford, *Sailmaker;* E. Brown, Jr., *Captain's Clerk;* Henry A. Mitchell, *Purser's Clerk.*

A few days after she was put into commission, Lieutenant Decatur died suddenly at the Naval Hospital. He was a brave officer, and his sudden death was lamented by all belonging to the ship. His place was supplied by the appointment of Lieutenant A. F. Warley, a smart and energetic officer. On the 19th of the same month, in a sudden squall, the ship broke adrift from her mooring opposite the Navy Yard, and ran afoul of what is called the Gas-House Wharf, injuring her port wheel so badly that it required thirty days' labor to repair the same. A court of inquiry was ordered to assemble at the Navy Yard, cf which Commodore Pendergrass was president, to investigate the cause of the accident; the result of which was that the court fully exonorated Captain Nicholson and his officers from all blame. By the great exertions of Mr. Danby, the repairs were carried on with all possible dispatch. During the accident, Captain Roots, of the Navy Yard, took some offence at our boatswain, and caused him to be put under an arrest, then reported him to the department; the result of which was, he was dismised from the service. Mr. Bates was a perfect sailor, and an excellent scholar; but, like many more of mankind, he was human, and had his faults. Mr. James McDonald, of Brooklyn, was immediately appointed in Bates's place.

Our ship's company consisted of thirty-one officers, forty-two marines, a band of twelve piece , forty-eight petty officers, twenty-nine seamen, forty-five ordinary seamen, thirty-five landsmen, fifteen boys, twenty-five firemen, twenty-five coal heavers; total, three hundred and seven souls.

On the 18th of August following, at eight, A.M., we steamed up, saluted our brother tars on board the "North Carolina" with three cheers, and left our moorings, and dropped down to the anchorage off the battery; there we took in our powder and loaded shells, and at sunrise the next morning started on our long cruise. As we passed down the bay, every one would peep through the ports, or steal up into the rigging, to catch a last glimpse of our own dear land. At ten, A.M., we discharged our pilot at the light-ship; and then, with a full head of steam on, we soon lost sight of American soil.

We were now fully at sea, and the ship was under strict martial law. Prayers were commenced morning and evening, and with few exceptions have been followed up the whole cruise. Services also have been held every Sunday forenoon, Captain Nicholson officiating, to which the crew have always cheerfully responded. Being clear from the land, the ship's course was shaped for Funchal, on the Island of Madeira, which was made in fifteen and a half days. The passage was a very pleasant and warm one. Three days previous to our arrival at the island, we spoke an English ship bound to London. By her we embraced the opportunity of sending letters home. The same day, large schools of dolphins were to be seen playing around the ship. We anchored in Funchal Roads at eleven, A.M., on the 4th of September. In port, we found the United States Sloop-of-War "Germantown," Commander Page, on her way from Norfolk to China, by the way of Bombay; also an English frigate, and six gun-boats, which were on their way from England to China. We remained at Funchal only six days, during which time we took in two hundred and fifty tons of coal, filled up with wood and water, and gave our boys all a run for twenty-four hours on shore. During our sojourn in the port, the American Consul, and others of note residing in the place, extended to Captain Nicholson and his officers every attention they could expect. Our men all behaved themselves well, and returned to the ship prompt and in good order. We hoisted the Portuguese flag at our fore, and saluted the town with twenty-one guns, which was returned from the fort, as usual, when a man-of-war enters the roadstead of Funchall. Our ship was surrounded by countless boats, containing washerwomen and compradores. And it matters not if you have never seen Madeira before, the old dames of washerwomen, as they climb over the sides of the ship, will grasp you by the hand, and insist upon having your washing, as each certainly washed for you when you were there last, although you had never seen the island before. One lively old dame, well known as Rose, — she will make you believe that she has washed for all the officers in the American Navy. And she is always so polite, and has such handsome, *genteel daughters*, who generally manage the laundry of her department, that she generally carries the day, and gets nearly all the washing from the ship. Rose is a genuine Portuguese woman, and has laid up quite a handsome little fortune. Old Sarsfield, as he is well known, is the compradore for American ships ; and he will never allow an American seaman to be abused, or get hard-up on shore, if he knows it. He is truly the American sailor's friend.' Such a thing as pilots are not known. In Madeira, every captain must be his own pilot.

The most notable object in Madeira is Loo Rock, which is a high rock about a quarter of a mile from the shore, the top of which is occupied for a fort, and is garrisoned by a few Portuguese soldiers. From this fort all salutes are fired ; and, when an approaching storm is coming on, a signal gun is fired from this fort to give warning to all the shipping to leave, as it is well known to all mariners, that, at certain times of the year, the harbor of Funchal is very dangerous for ships to remain at anchor during the heavy gales that visit the island. Next is the church of the Lady of the Mount, which is situated almost at the top of the highest peak on the island, nearly a mile above the level of the sea. From the ship it presents quite a handsome appearance ; but, when you approach it (which you have to do either on foot or in sledges draw by oxen, up over narrow roads ' which are neatly paved with small cobble-stones), you find nothing about the building to repay you your dollar for the ride up to the same. It is a plain building, having two steeples, one at each end of its front. It is in this temple or church that all public days are celebrated. On entering the building, you are met by rather a hard-looking customer of a priest, whose outer appearance looks as if soap and water were luxuries that were not often used at the Mount. The interior of the building presents to the visitors any quantity of gilding and ornaments, which shows pretty plainly that time and age are fast destroying them. It was a feast-day at the time of our visit. And, having seen enough of the church and its worshippers, we gave the dirty-looking priest an old-fashioned pistareen, and then re-entered our ox-team, and, at the rate of 2.40, returned to our quarters at the London Hotel. We visited the residence of our most excellent consul, Mr. March, of the firm of Howard & March. He is, in every sense of the word, a perfect gentleman. His house is always open to his countrymen, and is as free to the destitute seaman as it is to the masters of ships. He is beloved by all in the place. He is very charitable, and gives away yearly large amounts of money, clothing, &c., to the poor. He is reported as being very rich,— may he long live to enjoy the same ! The grape crop of the island is fast running out, and wine is becoming higher in price every year. The two principal hotels in the place are the London and French : either of them may be ranked as a third-rate New York hotel. The streets, as in all Portuguese and Spanish ports, are full of street beggars ; and, turn which way the traveller will, he is sure to be saluted with the very pleasant sound of "John, give me one penny." The hospital of Funchal is a very large structure, and, from its rusty appearance, it must have been built a great many years ; but every thing inside and outside of it is dirty and filthy. Over the front entrance is a massive block of stone, which bears the royal arms of Portugal. The next place visited was the prison, or calaboose. Accompanied by a soldier on guard, I was shown over this den of filth and criminals of both sexes, old and young, all mixed up together, and such a horrid sight of wretchedness I never before laid eyes on ; and I thanked God that I lived in a free and Christian country.

On the tenth of the same month, everybody being on board, and the officers having laid in a good supply of " Old Madeira," and the crew a plenty of oranges and bananas, and ten live bullocks for the use of all hands, we steamed up, hove up our mud-hooks, turned our beautiful stern towards the town, and stood off towards the south, taking in tow the " Germantown." At nine, P.M., a strong breeze springing up, we let go the hawser that held her to us; and she stood on under canvass, and we kept on our way for Saint Helena. The third day out we passed the Cape de Verd Islands. Off these islands we had a strong northeast blow; but our good old ship kept on just as steady as if Old Boreas had not been about. We had a very pleasant passage of twenty-three days to St. Helena. A regular routine of duty was daily performed, such as general quarters, exercising the divisions of small arms, and single-sticks, quarters morning and night, and occasionally quarters at midnight, — which generally creates considerable excitement. At no time on board of a ship-of-war is there so much excitement and confusion as there is when the music calls all hands to general quarters in the night-time. When this is to take place, no one is in the secret but the captain and first lieutenant. Then there is such a hurry in turning out, lashing up hammocks, hurrying on deck to get them stowed, so as to get to each one's quarters as soon as possible ; while the young gents who live aft have to fly round, and, for once in their lives, shoulder their own hammock, and lug it on deck. This all done — which is never allowed to occupy more than two minutes — the first lieutenant sings out through his speaking-trumpet in a voice of thunder, " Silence fore and aft!" Then commences the regular exercises, by the orders of the first lieutenant. The guns are cast loose, the magazines are opened, the powder-boys hurry in passing and repassing cartridge-boxes. The guns are worked by the crew, and the boarders and pikemen are called away to repel boarders; while the marines form a conspicuous part in covering the boarders and pikemen, and the sail-trimmers are called away to trim the sails. The ship's bell sounds the alarm of fire, which is a signal for the firemen to repair to the scene of danger. The fire-hose is placed upon the pumps, and the supposed fire is extinguished; when the word is passed in the same thundering voice to run out and secure ; which being done, a retreat is beat, and the hammocks are again piped down. This is all done in the short space of eight minutes.

On the passage we passed several schools of whales and porpoises, and arrived at St. Helena on the afternoon of the third day of October. Here we found several American whalers in port, who saluted us by dipping their colors as we passed them. We hoisted the English flag at our fore, and saluted the town with twenty-one guns, which was promptly returned from the fort. The commandant of the place, and the American Consul, Mr. Kimball, immediately came on board, and extended the civilities of the place to Captain Nicholson and his officers; and they were both honored with the usual salutes due their rank when they left the ship. Here our tars had another run on shore. In the bay or roadstead of St. Helena were lying three hulks of condemned American slavers, stripped of all their gear. The landing is at the mole, at one end of the small beach that lies at the extreme end of Jamestown; and a few minutes' walk brings you to the gate by which you enter the town, at which English sentinels, with muskets in hand, are stationed. Getting inside, a fine crooked hard-rolled gravelled street is before you. Near to the gate, on this street, is the English church, built of red granite, of which the island supplies large quantities. It is a very neat and well-arranged edifice, the interior of which is tastefully finished. On the steeple is a handsome clock, which can be seen from all the shipping that happens to be in front of the town. Near by this are the quarters for the guard, the governor's house, public offices, and a handsome public garden, well filled with choice trees and plants; also a large hotel, which bears the title of the "London Hotel." In the rear of this is the ascent to Ladder Hill, on the top of which is the highest fort on the island. It is reached by nearly six hundred steps, which are very handsomely cut in the side of the hill. From the top of this hill you can look down upon the settlement of the Chinese, who have left their own country to dwell on this solitary island in the middle of the South Atlantic Ocean. You also see the fine parade-ground, where the garrison is almost daily drilled. The top of this hill is about one thousand feet above the level of the sea. When we had reached the top of this hill, we were completely exhausted, and gladly accepted the invitation of an English officer to walk into his quarters and rest ourselves. We were very kindly treated by all connected with the garrison on Ladder Hill. From this hill one has also a fine view of Diana's Peak, towering hundreds of feet in the clouds above. The view seaward is beautiful. Look which way you will, you find yourself standing on a lonely island, surrounded by the blue sea, with now and then a passing ship, with her white sails spread to the breeze, or a steamer ejecting forth her black smoke from her smoke-stack, which add much to the beauty of the scenes of St. Helena. Our next visit was to that sacred spot, Longwood, the home for years of the great Napoleon. A half-hour's walk brought us into a narrow, crooked lane or path, with fir, cypress, and other ornamental trees on either side. At the end of this road or lane we came to a small valley, enclosed by a half-decayed fence, with the old sentry-box standing close by. Within this enclosure is the remains of the vault that contained the remains of the great man so many years, before they were removed to France in 1844. In the old sentry-box, which was still standing when we were there, the British sentinels kept their daily watch of regular fort duty over the illustrious dead, for the sole reason that England was either afraid of him in death, or feared that his remains might be stolen. There is a beautiful weeping-willow tree within the enclosure, the branches of which spread entirely over the vault, by which there is a plentiful spring of water constantly flowing. The vault is much decayed; and to descend into it an old ladder answers the purpose of steps. The cross-stones on which the coffin of the great man rested are still left, although most every visitor takes away a piece of the vault as a keepsake, — consequently the walls have become very much broken up. To enter the enclosure, the visitor is compelled to pay a small fee to an English official on duty at the gate. (By the way, it is now the property of France. What right have English subjects to demand a fee of those who may wish to visit what was once the grave of the greatest man France ever produced?) Report says that Napoleon always drank the water at the spring near his grave. Our next step was to visit the buildings assigned for his residence. A walk of fifteen minutes brought us in sight of an old, dilapidated story-and-a-half building, with a verandah on the front side of it, near which is the old guard-house and signal-tower. In this building the great man lived and died an exile. The room in which he breathed his last is used as a place for storage of grain; and a part of the building is now used as a temporary grist-mill, propelled by wind; and what were once handsome flower-gardens are now all torn up, and are used as a cow pasture. In the rear of this house is a beautiful little pond, in which it is said Napoleon had a large number of pet fish, and that daily, after he had finished his own dinner, he resorted to this pond to feed them. Before entering this enclosure, we were compelled to pay another fee for the privilege of looking at the premises. Several stones have been removed from that part of the room in which the illustrious man died, and taken to France by order of the French government, as valuable keepsakes. Not far distant from this building stands the new house which was built for him; but he never entered it more than once or twice, and the English could not prevail upon him to move into it. The English at Jamestown cannot bear to hear a foreigner mention the name of the great man whom their country so cruelly treated; and well may they be ashamed of it. During our stay here parties were given by the officers of both governments. Our English friends done all they could to make our stay as agreeable as possible.

Here we took in coal sufficient to fill up our bunkers, and then filled up our tanks with water, and paid up all our bills; and on the tenth we steamed up (and sending down our topgallant-mast), hove up our anchor, and left the port, and stood on our way for Capetown, which port we reached on the twenty-first, after a very pleasant passage of eleven days. In this port we found the American clipper-ship "Gamecock," of Boston, with coals for our ship. We immediately hoisted the English flag at our fore, and saluted the town with twenty-one guns, which was returned from the fort. Our consul, George Holmes, came off to us, and was saluted with seven guns. We immediately commenced taking in our coal. During our stop, several English transport-ships, on their way to China and India with troops, put into the port for supplies; and the usual civilities were exchanged between their officers and our own. At that port, our men again had another run on shore. All the officials of the place paid us a visit, and they were received with the proper salutes due their respective ranks. Dinner-parties and balls were freely given on both sides, and our stay at Capetown was very pleasant.

On the morning of the thirty-first, we left Capetown, and shaped our course for the Indian Ocean : we had a very pleasant run, and by sundown same day we were fairly in that ocean. At Capetown, five of our men deserted. They were that class of men that could be easily spared out of ships of war, being too lazy to work or steal ; and most likely they starved to death in Capetown. Their shipmates were glad to get rid of them, that we might get good men in their places. On the third day of November we soon found out that we were really in the Indian Ocean, by being treated to a regular old-fashioned north-west gale, which lasted two days ; but our good old ship paid but little attention to it, and jogged along at the rate of five knots per hour.

The rest of the passage was quite pleasant, to Mauritius, Isle of France, at which port we arrived on the fourteenth of November. We found no American ships in port. We hoisted the English flag, and saluted the town with wenty-one guns, which was returned from the fort. The American, French, and Dutch consuls, also the governor of the place, visited the ship, and were received with salutes, &c. At this port it became our painful duty to commit to Mother Earth the first one of our number, John Schmidt, a member of our band. He died of consumption. He was followed to the grave by the petty officers, and a number of the crew, several marines, and several of our officers in full uniform ; the band playing the Dead March from " Saul." Thousands of the natives of the place followed our deceased shipmate to his last resting-place, being attracted to do so by the military appearance of the funeral cortege, and the music from the band. At the grave, three volleys were fired, and a suitable head-stone (of wood) marks the spot where John Schmidt, of the " Mississippi," now sleeps. The principal port of Mauritius is well known as Port Louis. The harbor is not very large, and in it are many rocks and shoals ; and, by a regulation of the port, all ships must lay moored head and stern. For this purpose, a pilot and the harbor-master board you, as soon as you are off the entrance of the harbor ; and they take charge, and moor the ship in such position as they may best judge. The trade carried on in the port is very extensive ; and, when we laid there, there were nearly one hundred vessels in port. Near to the town is a floating chapel, which is under the protection of the English Missionary Society ; it is free to seamen of all nations. The chaplain, the Rev. Mr. Watson, with his family, reside on board of her. The town is not very large ; but it presents quite a pretty appearance from the ships in the harbor, with the tall volcanic hills in the rear. The population is made up of English, French, Dutch, Greeks, Chinamen, Native Indians, Negroes; also Lascar and Malabar Indians, male and female, who are brought there by the English Government from India, and sold into slavery for five years, at the rate of four dollars per month. These people do all the labor on the plantations, in the same manner as the negroes of our southern states do: they are tall, well-built people, and are very strong, and capable of enduring a great deal of hardship. Sugar is raised to a very great extent at this island, — from one to two hundred millions of pounds are annually shipped from Port Louis. Monsieur I. Choran, a French gentleman, showed our officers every attention, and at his own expense took them all out to his very extensive sugar-plantation, about twenty-five miles into the interior: his income is said to be five hundred thousand dollars per year. The Lascar portion of the community, females, as well as males, go almost in a perfect state of nudity, wearing only a cotton cloth around their loins, which generally extends down to their knees. They are very numerous; and the garrison are obliged to keep a pretty sharp look-out for them for fear of a revolt among them. So strict are the laws of the place, that, if you happen to be out after eight o'clock, P. M., no one will open their doors to let you in; and the consequence is, you must take up lodgings in the guard-house, or return to your ship. The landing of the port is effected by some very nice stone steps: a few steps from the same and you are in a very fine park, well shaded with various trees. Near by are to be found cabs, and all sorts of looking teams, ready to convey you to any part of the island, or out to that noted spot, the tomb of Paul and Virginia. At the head of this park stands the palace of the governor of the island: it is an odd-looking structure, having many crooks and turns about its construction. The barracks of the port covers over several acres of ground, and is enclosed either by stone buildings or high walls; the quarters for the troops are around the sides of this enclosure, which leaves the whole area open for a fine parade-ground. There are several hotels in the place, but of a very inferior kind, ranking perhaps No. 4 New York houses. Religions, such as the English, Congregational, Catholic, Mahommedanism, Buddhism, Hindoo, &c., are all tolerated by the government. The Indians are permitted to marry as many wives as they think fit: frequently girls of nine and ten years of age are married to an ugly-looking Lascar, who has then three or four wives. The streets are wide and very clean, and are ornamented with blocks of handsome stores, which are occupied by merchants, &c.

Our coal being all on board, and every thing ready for sea, we left Port Louis early in the morning of the twenty-first day of November, and shaped our coarse for Batavia, through the Straits of Sunda. Every thing passed off very pleasant on this passage, until the third day of December, when we encountered a heavy south-east gale, which lasted for fifty-three hours. A part of the time it blew a perfect hurricane, the wind howling through our rigging in a most mournful manner; but the good ship braved the storm well, while our old hero of a captain, backed by a noble set of tars, stood ready for any emergency. We found several spars with some rigging attached to them. The sea was running, during the whole time, to a frightful height. We rode it out in good style, without sustaining any damage. On the seventh, we had the second part of this gale, which lasted thirty-six hours, with a tremendous ugly sea on, which gave us such a terrible knocking about that it caused several of our green ones to throw up, pretty freely, their allowance of whiskey and salt-horse. These were the first blows that we had experienced during our whole passage from New York, and made a number of our land-lubbers wish that they were at home again. John Schebel, the master of the band,— poor fellow! — was so much alarmed that he would kneel down and try to pray. And, on several occasions during the blow, he said he would jump overboard : when asked for what, " Why," says he, " the ship will sink, and I don't want to *go down in her ;* " but kind Providence spared our ship and him too.

On the eleventh, the good old " Mississippi " was logged eleven knots under steam alone, which was considered as great work for her. On the twelfth, we made Java Head ; entered the Straits of Sunda at eight, A. M At ten, A. M., run into Muse Bay, to see if the ship with coal for us was in there : found nothing but a few fishermen, who left their frail crafts and run up the hills as if the Old Nick was after them, when they saw us heave in sight. At five, P. M., same day, anchored off Anjier Point; blowing very fresh at the time, could not communicate with the shore. Next morning, the wind and sea subsiding, a Dutch official came off in a canoe pulled by some Malays, to tender the respects of the governor of the little town to Captain Nicholson, and to ascertain if we were in want of any thing; being answered in the negative, he retired. Shortly afterwards, a bumboat came off well filled with fowls, eggs, and fruit ; and all hands had a glorious blow-out. Next day, Sunday, it blew almost a gale ; both anchors down. An English ship came to near us, with loss of main-topmast ; offered her assistance, which was declined. Fourteenth, wind abated ; got under weigh, and proceeded up to Batavia ; anchored at half-past four, P. M., same day There we found the ship " Harry of the West " waiting for us, with coal for our ship. Next morning at eight o'clock hoisted the Dutch flag, and saluted the town with twenty-one guns, which was returned from the fort ; saluted also the Dutch Admiral with thirteen guns, which was returned from his ship. No communication with the shore, owing to the sickly state of the country. Commenced taking in coal. Took from the Admiral's ship the following men, who had deserted from the " Minnesota :" Robert Baily, I. S. Rogers, William Cannin, John McNerpy, Robert Maghin, and William Childs. The surgeon and his comical steward were called upon on several occasions to render assistance to the sick American seamen of the " Harry of the West," and other American ships, which was promptly done without any regard of danger or expense to themselves. Set up our rigging and tarred down. Weather extremely hot; glass in the shade, on shipboard, at 94°.

On the twenty-fourth, hove up, having our coal on board, and left

Batavia. The twenty-fifth being Christmas-day, all hands were called to "splice the main-brace" (which is to take a tot of whiskey at government expense); at five, P. M., anchored in the Straits of Bancher, loaded the marines' muskets with ball-cartridges, so as to repel any attack from the natives (Malays) of the surrounding islands, who sometimes venture to attack ships that happen to anchor near their shores at night. At sunrise next morning hove up the anchor, and proceeded up the straits till sundown, when we again anchored in the same straits. Left the straits at sunrise next morning, and anchored at Singapore at three, P. M., on the twenty-ninth, and the next day saluted the town with twenty-one guns, which was returned from the shore. We also saluted the American and British Consuls with seven guns each. Here we painted the ship, &c.

Singapore is a free port, and is under the English rule. The inhabitants are composed of men from all parts of the globe, the Chinese being in the majority. There is nothing of much note to be seen in the town, unless it is the dirty streets and temples, which last bear the marks of age, and are pretty well ornamented with images, &c. The Hindoo temple is by far the most interesting one in the place, to enter which the visitor is required to take off his shoes. A large trade is carried on at this port, and a great number of ships of all nations are always in the harbor.

We left our presents for the King of Siam in the care of the American consul, and left the port on the morning of the second day of January, 1858, and proceeded on our way to Hong Kong, against very strong north-east monsoons, and more or less rain every day.

On the eleventh, took on board a Chinese pilot; weather very thick and foggy. At sundown, "Land, ho!" and "Breakers ahead!" was sung out by the look-outs. Immediately backed ship off, and anchored at eight and a half, P. M. In ten minutes more the good old ship "Mississippi" would have been hard and fast among the breakers of one of the islands forming the cluster of islands around Hong Kong. At the time of discovering land, the weather was very thick and heavy. It was therefore impossible to tell where we were, as the fool of a pilot we had on board did not know where we were himself; and had it not been for the cool and firm manner in which Captain Nicholson, and the master, Mr. George Bacon, worked the ship off, and out of danger, she would undoubtedly have been lost; and perhaps not one of her crew would have been left to tell of the misfortune of the good old "Mississippi." Next day we got under weigh, and proceeded up to Hong Kong. As we hove in sight of the shipping, we discovered the "San Jacinto," "Minnesota," and "Portsmouth," at anchor. We immediately saluted Commodore Armstrong with thirteen guns, — which was returned from the "San Jacinto," — and anchored at Hong Kong at eleven, A. M., having made the run from New York to that port in ninety-nine and a half sailing days. Here our hearts were made glad by receiving letters and papers from our friends, being the first we had received for nearly five months. The next day hoisted our flags at half-mast, and fired at noon thirteen minute guns in respect to the memory of the late Commodore T. I. Newton Purser T. B. Looker, who went out passenger with us for duty on board the "Portsmouth," immediately joined that ship. A better man never walked a ship's quarter-deck than Purser Looker; he is a Christian of the right stamp, and a friend to the sailor. May his days be long on earth, to do good to his brother sailors and mankind!

On the fourteenth, Hon. William B. Reed, Minister to China, visited the ship, and was received by Captain Nicholson and all of his officers, in full uniform; and the marines presented arms, while the band performed the favorite air of "Hail, Columbia!" This over, he was then honored with a salute of seventeen guns. The honorable gentleman proceeded from our ship to the English seventy-four the "Princess Charlotte," where he was also saluted with the same number of guns.

On the fifteenth, Commodore Josiah Tatnall, accompanied by his son as secretary, arrived in the oriental mail steamer, and took up his quarters on board the "Portsmouth."

On the eighteenth, a general court-martial was convened on board the "Mississippi," of which Captain S. F. Dupont was appointed president, for the trial of Lieut. A. F. Warley, on charges preferred against him by Capt. Nicholson; also for the trial of a seaman for assaulting Sergeant Block, of the marines (who by the way is a native of Poland, and can hardly speak the English language; yet he was made a sergeant in our marine guard by Gen. Henderson, before he had been six months in the country, when there were several good men—*Americans!*—who had for years been in the same service). Block first insulted the seaman, and provoked the assault. For this he was tried and convicted: the Court took into consideration the provocation given, and sentenced the prisoner to only thirty days' confinement. It is a disgrace to our service to have it known that the marine corps of our service is nearly all foreigners. Some of them are very excellent men; but most certainly the non-commissioned officers should be chosen from among those of our own countrymen who may choose to enter that branch of the service, and not to foreigners who have no claim upon the country. Lieut. Warley was acquitted of a part of the charges preferred against him, and was sentenced to be reprimanded by Captain Nicholson, and to go to his duty again. Lieut. Warley is a brave and generous officer, and was well liked by all the crew.

On the nineteenth, we joined in a general salute in honor of the birth-day of the Duchess of the Netherlands.

On the twentieth, we hoisted the English flag at our fore, and saluted Admiral Sir Michael Seymour with thirteen guns, which was returned from his ship, the "Calcutta." Captain Nicholson and his officers, as is generally the custom when a new ship first arrives on the station, were feasted by their English friends. Governor Sir John Bowring honored them also with a grand dinner-party.

It is useless for me to say much about Hong Kong, as no doubt most of my readers have been there; and those that have not have already read various accounts in the papers, and books that have been published respecting the place. I will only say, that, to my eye, it is a most miserable, filthy hole, and fit only for dirty John Chinaman to live in. As to beauty, I was at a loss to find any thing about the town worthy of note. I consider the residence of Messrs. Russell & Co., American bankers, the only fine building in the town. The barracks, to be sure, cover a great deal of waste ground; but they present nothing interesting to the beholder, unless it is the skeletons walking about alive in the shape of red-coat troops, whose countenances show that the various diseases of the climate have made their mark upon them. The English church near by these buildings is an odd-looking affair, with all sorts of corners; and there is a bell in it to summon the troops and others to worship, which reminds me of a cow-bell that my old grandfather used to attach to his cows, when he sent them adrift to feed on the highways free of charge. Dissipation is carried on in the place to an alarming extent. *Whoredom* and *drunkenness* have there complete sway, and rum-holes (or "murdering-shops," as I shall style them) are as thick as they can well be packed together. It is almost certain ruin for the young sailor who may accidentally get "hard up" and astray in Hong Kong. The landlords of the countless sailor boarding-houses are nothing more or less than a gang of regular land-sharks and pirates, most of whom were driven out of California by the vigilance committee. I would advise all sailors going to Hong Kong to beware lest they should fall into the dens of these land-pirates.

At eleven o'clock, A. M., on the twenty-ninth of January, all the ships of our squadron manned their yards, and commodore James Armstrong hauled down his broad pennant on board of the frigate "San Jacinto," and she immediately fired a salute of thirteen guns. The commodore, accompanied by Surgeon William M. Wood, of that ship, and his secretary, left her, and went on board of the oriental mail steamer to take passage for home by the overland route; he being relieved at his own request, on account of ill-health. As the barge which contained him and his suite passed the "Mississippi," he was saluted with three cheers from our gallant tars, and the band playing "Hail to the Chief." The next day at eight, A. M., all the squadron fired a salute of thirteen guns; and Commodore Tatnall took charge of the squadron, and hoisted his flag on board of the "San Jacinto." After this, the English, French, and Dutch saluted our new commander-in-chief with thirteen guns, all of which were returned by the commodore. For eighteen hours we had the honor of being the flag-ship of the East India squadron. The same day, Governor Sir John Bowring visited the commodore, and was honored with a salute of seventeen guns. Same day, sent the starboard watch on shore for twenty-four hours' liberty; each man receiving ten dollars liberty-money.

On the first of February we steamed up, and proceeded with all possible dispatch to Macao, there to await the pleasure of Honorable Mr. Reed.

We supposed, — and no doubt it was so, — that we were sent down to intercept the clipper ship " Flora Temple," loaded with coolies, and to prevent her sailing ; but before we got orders from Mr. Reed how to proceed, the captain of the " Flora Temple " took advantage of the darkness of the night, and a fair breeze, and left us to find him if we could; and, when the day broke, the " Flora Temple," coolies and all, had flown. Next day after our arrival, we hoisted the Portuguese flag at our fore, and saluted it with twenty-one guns, which was returned from the fort.

On the third day we took the Honorable Mr. Reed and his son on board, and left Macao, and returned to Hong Kong, arriving there the same afternoon. As we hove in sight, Commodore Tatnall saluted Mr. Reed with seventeen guns. We then sent the port watch on shore, on liberty for the same length of time as the starboard went for. When their time expired, they all returned to the ship in good order, and promptly, gaining for themselves a good name for their orderly conduct while on shore.

On the eighth, the frigate " San Jacinto " left for a cruise and a visit to Manilla. On the tenth, the " Minnesota," with Mr. Reed on board, sailed for Macao.

While speaking of Macao, perhaps a few remarks respecting the place may not come amiss at this time. It is well known to all, that the island of which this town forms a part was ceded to the Portuguese government, a great many years ago, for valuable services rendered by the Portuguese to China. The town at a distance, in shape, looks very much like an amphitheatre. The dwellings and stores are entirely different from, and of much handsomer construction than, those of Hong Kong, or any other port of China, with wide verandas in front of them, to protect the occupants from the hot sun in the warm season. A large proportion of the population are Chinese ; the next most numerous are the Portuguese, with a scattering of English, American, French, and Dutch. Numerous garrisons, batteries, and queer-looking forts protect the place. From a flag-staff erected on one, flies daily the Portuguese flag. The water, as you approach the island, shoals very fast; and vessels of much draught cannot lie very near to the principal landing, which is effected by a flight of handsome stone steps, like other ports in China. The boats, or san-pans, are manned by women and young girls, who, with their handsome teeth and breeches, with hair nicely plaited, and small, bare feet, surround the ship; and as one goes over the rail they all set up the cry, " My boat, sir! my boat, sir!" Near Franch's Hotel, on the praya, near the principal promenade ground, all the gentility of the place resort to take an evening walk, and to enjoy the sea breeze. Macao is a much better place to find good society than Hong Kong; yet, like all other parts of China, it has its miseries, — *rum* and *houses of doubtful reputation* are as plenty as they are in Hong Kong. A steamer plies daily between the two places, — distance sixty miles, fare three dollars, without meals. The Rev. S. Wells Williams, American missionary, resides at Macao. He was one of Mr. Reed's legation. The coolie trade is carried

2

on on a very extensive scale from that port, the Portuguese government throwing no obstacle in the way of the traders engaged in this unlawful traffic.

On the twelfth, our marines and band of music went on shore, to escort the remains of John Pritty, a private marine, who had died at the hospital, to the American burial-ground, in Happy Valley. He was attached to the "San Jacinto," which being absent, this duty devolved upon us. He died with diarrhœa.

Early on the morning of the following day, the chartered steamer "Antelope" brought a dispatch for us to proceed at once to Shanghae; and we immediately steamed up, and left in the afternoon, and arrived in the Yangtzee-Kiang on the afternoon of the twentieth, being seven days on the passage. The monsoons being against us, we had a very rough and cold passage, being obliged to run against a very ugly sea. We came in contact with a Chinese junk, and took her spars out of her; no one injured. Early next morning we left the river, and, with a pilot on board, proceeded up to Woosung, and came to an anchor at eleven, A.M.; the weather being very cold. We could not go up to Shanghae, owing to the plain fact that our steamer drew too much water. The twenty-second being the anniversary of the birth-day of the Father of his Country, at eight, A.M., we draped the ship with extra colors; and at twelve o'clock, noon, we fired a national salute of twenty-one guns. The twenty-sixth, forty Chinese pirates were publicly beheaded at Shanghae for piracy. They had been previously captured by a Chinese war-steamer, and tried, and condemned to be beheaded; after which their heads were placed in cages, and, by order of the imperial code of law, they were hung up on trees in the public roads, as a warning to others. Our ship was surrounded by about two hundred junks, that had run in to make a harbor from an approaching storm; and these junks being illuminated every Saturday night, and their "chin-chin-ing for Josh," assisted us much to pass away the cold and disagreeable time. The river being fresh water, we filled up our tanks with the same.

The writer took one flying visit on shore, to see the sights of Woosung. One visit was enough. As I approached the town in a san-pan, my eyes beheld one mass of dirty, filthy looking buildings, all crowded together, with here and there a "Josh-House" peeping up from the rest. On landing, my nostrils were well filled with the fumes of opium, and other offensive articles which decency requires that I should omit mentioning. I found the streets very narrow, and filthy shops, dirtier than a well-managed pig-sty in a country village; while the Chinamen clustered around me in large numbers, eager to catch a glimpse of an *American* outside *barbarian*. As my whiskers were extremely long, I presume that they took me for some wild man. As it was, they were very civil towards me, and did not attempt to show me the least insult. On the other hand, had they been so disposed, they could have taken my head off; and no one would have been able to have told what had become of the "Mississippi's" surgeon's steward. The

Chinamen of Woosung expressed, as far as I had any thing to say to them, a good feeling for our countrymen; but "English," they remarked, "was no good."

As to Shanghae, I can only say, that part which is occupied outside of the gates by European consuls and merchants is a tolerably decent neighborhood. It supports two hotels, and a sailors' home. In China, towns like those of Woosung and Shanghae are miserable holes; yet some of the Chinese residing therein are immensely rich, and worth their millions. The ship was here supplied with fruit, from Old Smilly's bumboat; and, like Old Sam, the bumboat man at Hong Kong, they are making a handsome fortune out of the tars of Uncle Sam's ships-of-war who visit China. The Chinese, like all other parts of the world, had rather see a Yankee man-of-war in their ports than any other, for the well-known reason that they spend more money than any other nation. Directly in front of the ship could be seen, hung up in trees, cages containing the heads (with their long tails hanging thereto) of some of those Chinese who had been decapitated for some violation of the high imperial laws of their country. At Woosung, they bury no dead in the earth. They are placed in coffins made straight out of plank, of four and six inches thick. They are then taken to some selected spot by the relatives of the deceased one. There stakes are driven into the ground, cross-pieces are then secured to the stakes, on which the coffin containing the defunct Chinaman is placed, and there left exposed to all storms and weather, until the whole shall, by the process of time, become decayed; and, as the plank used in the construction of the coffin is a very hard Chinese wood, almost similar to our live oak, it requires a number of years to rot it. I saw two or three which had begun to decay, and, from the looks of them, they must have been exposed this way a number of years. The end of one was so far gone that I could look into it, and it exposed to my view a few human bones, entirely deserted of all flesh, &c. At Woosung River lie American and English opium hulks, well filled with the deadly poison, which they force upon the Chinese at most exorbitant prices. They are all well guarded with officers and men; and each bulk is supplied with heavy guns, shot, and ammunition, to protect them from any attack from the Chinese or pirates, of whom the neighborhood of Shanghae, Woosung, and the rivers adjoining, are full. Most of the deeds that they commit are generally upon their own countrymen.

On the eighth we hove up the anchor, and left Woosung River, in charge of an English pilot, and anchored again at sundown, on the river. We had on board the English Consul of Shanghae, who, being in delicate health, wished to go to Manilla, for the benefit of his health. Captain Nicholson very generously gave him a passage, and free use of his cabin. As we passed the Chinese ship-of-war "Glenion" (an old English barque), she saluted us by dipping her colors. At six, A.M., next day, got under weigh; at ten, A.M., discharged the pilot, and sent him on board of the light-ship. Captain Nicholson gave a grand dinner-party to the English Consul and his officers; ship going at nine knots, with steam and canvass. In the afternoon went to general quarters. I might as well state now, that we went to quarters every night and morning, and to general quarters (when we went through a sham battle) once every week. Saturday was always the day, when the weather would admit of the same, for airing bedding; and the day was given to the men to mend their clothing, &c. At sundown, always had what is termed fire quarters, which is this: the ship is supposed to be on fire; and, when the fire-bell rings, all hands go to their quarters, and the fire apparatus are all prepared for extinguishing the supposed fire; that done, a retreat is beat. Two of our lads were confined for a short time this afternoon, in the cells, for disobedience of orders.

Passed the American steamer "Yangtazee," which plies between Hong Kong and Shanghae. At four, P.M., a large sail in sight. Arrived at Manilla at half-past five, P.M., on the sixteenth; having had a very hot passage, with large quantities of rain. The captain of the port, a hard-looking Spaniard, came off, and ascertained who we were, and where from, and extended the hospitalities of the place to our captain and officers. Here we were all doomed to disappointment, as we had made up our minds for a long stop in that port, and have a fine time ashore. But, when the purser returned from the shore, he brought a dispatch, which the commodore had left for us, which was to the effect that we must leave in forty-eight hours after our arrival, proceed to Hong Kong, take in coal and provisions, and join him at Shanghae by the first of April; which order we all wished the old commodore had kept to himself, for it knocked all our plans into a cocked hat. Captain Nicholson could not be prevailed upon to stop any longer. Accordingly, the next morning, a few of the officers went up to the town. We hoisted the Spanish flag at our fore, and saluted the town with twenty-one guns, which was returned from the fort. Here we found the weather exceedingly hot and oppressive. Took on board three men, who had deserted from the frigate "Minnesota," during her visit to this place. They had been previously arrested by the police, and confined in the calaboose.

On the eighteenth, at eight, A.M., hove up anchor, and, under steam and canvass, left Manilla; ship going nine knots. Purser paid out monthly money of five dollars to all hands. The twenty-first was a very rough and disagreeable day; wind ahead, blowing almost a gale, and a very heavy sea running. The ship being light, she rolled a great deal, causing at times pots, pans, &c., to roll about the decks, to the amusement of all. Made land at six, P.M. The weather coming up very thick, we put the ship about, and stood off the land. At daylight next day stood in for the land; made out the Island of Macao at eight, A.M. At twelve o'clock, noon, took on board a Chinese pilot, and stood in for the south channel. Shortly afterwards we passed a sunken wreck, barque-rigged; her topmast was out of the water, with topgallant yards across. At six, P.M., anchored in the channel; weather very cold and disagreeable.

Next morning, at five, A.M., left the channel; proceeded to Hong Kong, and anchored at nine, A.M. Found none of our squadron in port. Heard the news of the capture of William Walker, the land-pirate, at Nicaragua. Saluted the French admiral with thirteen guns, which was returned from his ship. Commenced taking in coal and provisions. Twenty-fifth, Admiral Seymour sails in the "Calcutta" seventy-four gun ship for the North. Twenty-sixth, a large fire broke out in that part of Hong Kong known as Chinatown, which destroyed between fifty and sixty buildings, all of which were occupied by Chinese for shops and dwellings. Considerable property was also destroyed besides the buildings. The master of the American clipper ship "Norway," of New York, gave a grand dinner-party to Capt. Nicholson. Our band, led by Schebel, furnished the music for the occasion. Our men were allowed to have a run on shore, the coal and provisions being all on board.

On the twenty-seventh, at ten, A.M., our steam being up, and our tars all being on board (excepting Henry Ellsworth, a worthless mulatto, and Francis Grimes, a worthless Irish chap), we left Hong Kong and the two deserters behind. Two seamen were confined in irons for resisting their superior officers, who were sent on shore to bring them off to the ship. Thirtieth, a summary court-martial, composed of Lieutenants Stemble, Warley, and Esben, and Purser Nalle, convened in the captain's cabin, to try the two above-named seamen. In the afternoon, passed a large steamer; hundreds of junks all around us. Between forty and fifty men stopped their rations of grog. Thirty-first, court-martial finished their session. The steamer still in sight; she proved to be the "Coromandel," English tender to Admiral Seymour, her officers doing their best to pass us. Great excitement is produced in regard to the race. Our chief engineer, Mr. Danby, orders an extra bucket of coal or so to be put into the furnace. We leave her fast astern. All of a sudden she stops, and blows off her steam. We go about, and run down to her, to ascertain if she has met with any accident. We near her, and hail. The answer is, "No, I thank you; we have some slight repairs to make." We bid him good afternoon, and kept on our way, satisfied that they acknowledged the "corn," and gave up beat.

April first.—During a thick fog last night, we came in contact with a Chinese junk, damaging her some. We also came near having a serious collision with the steamer "Yangtazee," which was only avoided by our quarter-master of the watch putting the helm hard down, just in season to escape her. At eleven, A.M., all hands called to muster, to hear the doings of the court-martial read, which was: one of the prisoners was sentenced to be disrated, loose three months' pay, and be deprived of liberty for six months; the other was sentenced to thirty days' confinement on bread and water, and be deprived of liberty for one year, — one-half of the thirty days to be confined in the *cells*, or *sweat-boxes.* On the second, we took a pilot. At six, P.M., discovered an unknown steamer, running towards us. We immediately backed our ship, and stopped our engines. Still the steamer came on, until she struck us, carrying away our jib-boom, and doing some other slight damage. We immediately came to anchor, and called all hands to clear the wreck; and before midnight we had the broken boom on board, and a new one rigged in its place. The unknown steamer also anchored. She had, by the accident, her main yard and mizzen-topmast carried away. During the night she left, without even letting us know who she was.

Next day, at twelve o'clock, noon, hove up, and proceeded on our way to Woosung; anchored at four, P.M. If cursing ever sent a poor fellow to that bad place so much spoken of, the officer in command on board of that steamer would have been badly off, if the curses of some of our old tars had had much effect. On the following day, Commodore Josiah Tatnall, who, with his ship, was waiting our arrival, came on board of us. On our way up the river, we passed the "Minnesota" at anchor outside the bar, fifteen miles from Shanghae; she drawing too much water to proceed any further up. Delivered up to her the three deserters which we took on board at Manilla. Learned that the steamer that run into us was the French war-steamer "Fuse." Had a peep at her; she showed pretty plainly that she got the worst part of the bargain. Filled up with water out of the river. Rather dirty water, with now and then a dead Chinaman floating down the same. If any thing, we thought this gave the water a better relish. On the eighth, the frigate "San Jacinto" left for Hong Kong and the United States. Tenth, the English frigate "Furious" came down from Shanghae, having on board Lord Elgin, the English Minister, on his way to the mouth of the Peiho River. As she neared us, we hoisted the English flag at our fore, and saluted his lordship with nineteen guns, while the band saluted him with "God save the Queen." The "Furious" had a gunboat alongside of her in tow, and for that reason his lordship expressed his regret that he could not return our salute. In the afternoon, the purser's clerk and a midshipman had a set-to, in the shape of a little fight, and the "middy" got the worst part of the bargain. For this unruly conduct on the part of young gentlemen, they were reprimanded by the captain, and told to "go and sin no more." On the eleventh, hoisted the cornet to summon all hands on board of the ship; all going out of the ship prohibited.

Next day, at ten, A.M., the chartered American steamer "Antelope" came down from Shanghae, with the American ensign flying at her fore, denoting that the Honorable William Reed, United States Minister, &c., was on board. We sent the barge and third cutter alongside of her, to convey the distinguished gentleman and his suite to the "Mississippi." He was received on board with all the honor due his rank; and the American ensign was forthwith hoisted at our main.

Took a pilot on board, and a junk, called the "Peiho," in tow, and at half-past ten got under weigh and left the river, passing the "Minnesota," and an English and French frigate. It was expected they would salute our distinguished passenger, a compliment with which we honored Lord Elgin when he passed down the river by us; but, from some unknown cause, they did not. At half-past six, P.M., we discharged the pilot. Weather very thick and cold. Next day, formed a company of volunteer riflemen, forty-five in number. J. W. Kelley (midshipman) appointed captain ; Oliver F. Taylor and Sherman Church appointed sergeants. This company was formed at the suggestion of Mr. Reed, to act as his escort in the vicinity of Peiho, if it should be deemed necessary to have an escort ; he preferring to have blue-jackets rather than marines. This company was daily drilled, and their ma-nœuvres were equally as well gone through with as those of the marines ; and that is saying a great deal, for our marine-guard was a well-drilled one, and a better drill-officer cannot be found than · Lieutenant Jacob Reed, our marine officer. His whole soul is enlisted in his duty ; besides, a better-hearted man never sailed on salt-water. He is a democrat to the back-bone. He believes that one man is as good as another. Mr. Reed's suite consisted of the Rev. S. Wells Williams, secretary to the Legation ; A. McKinley, private secretary ; William B. Reed, Jr., attaché ; and a China-man, as translator.

We anchored in the Gulf of Pachelie, eight miles from the mouth of the Peiho River. On our passage, all hands were daily drilled at the big guns, and in small arms, anticipating that we might be called upon to show some of our skill in the vicinity of Peiho. We also had target-practice daily, and the way the targets were cut up showed that we had some excellent marks-men on board. In the gulf, we found the English frigate " Furious " at anchor, with Lord Elgin on board ; three English gun-boats ; one French frigate ; and the Russian frigate " America," on board of which was Count Poutatian, the Russian Minister to China, who was also commander-in-chief of the Russian forces in the Chinese waters. This was on Saturday. The weather was very boisterous and cold. Next afternoon (Sunday), Count Poutatian came on board of us to see Mr. Reed, and remained on board until Monday morning. Most of this time the two ministers were in private consultation. His boat's-crew of hearty-looking Russian seamen were well provided for by our warm-hearted tars, who always are ready to lend their aid to a brother sailor.

On the nineteenth, two high red-ball mandarins came down from Peiho in a junk, to ascertain the cause of our visit to that quarter. They were very polite and civil, and seemed highly delighted when told that we came there as friends, and as Americans, and shook Captain Nicholson and all warmly by the hand. They were then introduced to Mr. Reed by Mr. Williams, with whom they had a long conversation, through the interpreter. Captain Nicholson had some hot coffee furnished for them and their attend-ants, about twenty in number. The weather being very cold, this kind act of our warm-hearted captain pleased them very much. Mr. Reed assured them that our visit was one of friendship, peace, and commerce, and that we did not come there as enemies, but as American friends. Mr. Reed in-formed them that he had a dispatch to send to the emperor, and that our little junk. the " Peiho," was about starting up to the forts to deliver it. The mandarins offered to furnish any provisions we might want free of cost.

To this Mr. Reed objected, stating that we must pay for all that we received from them. They also thought that our letter would be received without any difficulty. They then gave Mr. Reed and the officers another shake of the hand, and, and, bowing very politely, left the ship.

The little " Peiho " was then hauled alongside; provisions and water for three days were put on board of her. Sailing-master George Bacon, in charge, aided by midshipmen J. W. Kelly, T. B. Mills, and James Pritchett, with three petty officers and one boy, composed the officers and crew of her; Drs. D. B. Phillips, T. S. Wales, Lieut. Jacob Reed, Assistant Engineers Williams and Bartleman, being invited by Mr. Bacon to accompany him. His orders were to proceed up to the Peiho, and sound on the bar and its vicinity, but not to venture too far in shore, and, if possible, get some one to take the letter in charge, to be conveyed to the emperor. With these instructions, the expedition left the ship, and proceeded towards the mouth of the river. Crossing the bar, they kept on up to the forts; and, not being able to send their letter on shore by any one, this little but brave party of Americans decided to face the lion in his den; and accordingly they kept on until they were well up the river, with the guns of three forts on one side and those of two on the other side of them pointing directly at them. As they neared the shore, the Chinese mustered down to the beach in thousands. The guns, three hundred in number, were brought to bear upon the little " Peiho "; the matches were lit, ready to be communicated to the loaded guns: but the little party kept on until they came near to the beach. There they were met by a large party of mandarins, with hundreds of Chinese troops drawn up in a line. The mandarins ordered them off; but the party paid no attention to this order, and gave them to understand that they had a letter for the emperor, which must be delivered to a responsible person or persons, to be delivered to him; and that, unless such a person did come and take the same, they would, in spite of all their military display, land, and deliver the same to the proper officer at the fort. After some hesitation, finding that our little but brave party were determined to carry their point, the proper officers came; and, after considerable pow-wowing, concluded to take the letter, promising to have it sent to the emperor at Pekin. They then requested our party to leave the river. It being night, and the tide too low to cross the bar, Mr. Bacon gave them to understand that they should remain in the river over night, or until the tide suited to cross the bar; and the little " Peiho," in defiance of loaded guns, troops, &c., anchored for the night directly under three hundred guns, mounted on four forts, and manned at least by ten or fifteen thousand troops. It was easy to be seen, during that eventful night, that the Chinese were in continual motion, watching the little party on board of the small schooner junk. It was a hard and dangerous night to pass over. Sleep was not enjoyed much on board of her, and daylight was welcomed by all the party, — when they left the river, and returned to the ship, fairly worn out, but fully satisfied, that, as true Americans, they had done their duty faithfully, at the immediate risk of their lives. The above forts were all dressed off in the most gaudy style, with flags and streamers of every fanciful color ; while the red, white, and black ball cap mandarins, with their silk gowns and trowsers, made a most singular appearance. In the river, at a good distance off from the forts, and out of the range of the guns of the same, the English were busily engaged in sounding, and laying down buoys along the channel which was to be the passage of the gun-boats of the allies up to the scene of action.

During our stop in the gulf (which was any thing but pleasant; the weather all the time being very cold, with a strong wind blowing off shore, sending forth and filling the air with a red dust or sand to such a degree that at times it was almost impossible to see the length of the ship ahead of her), the very best of good feeling prevailed between the ministers, officers and men of the different ships. Our leisure time was occupied at general quarters, fire quarters, exercising divisions in small arms, and target-exercises. On the twenty-first, we saluted the French Admiral with nineteen guns. The English frigate " Pique " also saluted him with the same number of guns. Both salutes were returned from the Admiral's ship. The ships-of-war and gun-boats of all the powers being increased to the additional arrivals, every thing in the gulf assumed quite a warlike appearance. On the twenty-second, the chartered steamer " Antelope " arrived from Shanghae ; and, much to the disappointment of all, she brought not one letter for any of us, which gave cause to a general bad feeling with all hands ; while some swore that they never would write again, others that their friend at home had forgotten them, &c., &c. A junk came down from the river with pigs, fowls, vegetables, eggs, and fruit, sent to us as a present, which we could not accept, the mandarins refusing to take pay for the same. Supplied the Russian frigate " America " with five hundred gallons of water. Twenty-fourth, sent the second cutter up to the forts, in charge of Lieutenant Henry Esben, to deliver a letter, which he did without any resistance. When his boat reached the beach, a high mandarin came to his boat, held a pow-wow with him, and took his letter. There is not the least doubt that our first expedition up to the forts was taken by the Chinese to be English in disguise with the American flag flying; for, after our arrival in the gulf was well known, they sent mandarins often to the ship, to see if we wanted any thing, — a favor, mind you, which they did not extend to the English and French.

On the twenty-fifth, four French ships-of-war arrived ; also the English seventy-four gun ship, " Calcutta," — Admiral Seymour's flag-ship. Filled up our tanks with two tons of water from the " Antelope." By an arrival of a gun-boat from Hong Kong, we received a letter-bag which gladdened many of our hearts, while some were doomed to grieve for the loss of some near and dear relative. There is nothing so joyful to the mariner, in a far-distant country, as to receive a letter from a fond wife and children ; or an aged parent, which brings to their distant son their prayers for his safety ; and to hear that all at home are well. Then, again, when one receives intelligence of the death of a fond wife, child, parent, brother, or sister, what a change comes over that individual! He seeks some secluded corner of the ship, and there alone gives vent to his feelings, and offers up a feeble prayer to heaven, — for sailors can pray, as bad as the majority of mankind believe they are. He goes about the ship solitary and alone; says nothing to no one; and his countenance is pictured with despair. I will here remark that it is to be hoped, that, as the men who now fill our ships-of-war are daily becoming better, it would be a most worthy undertaking for our benevolent people to see that they are fitted out with suitable libraries before they leave the United States, of the proper kind of books, for the sole use of the men. Government furnishes libraries in our ships; but they are for the exclusive use of the officers, and kept in the cabin, where no foremast hand can reach them. The frigate "Minnesota" arrived to-day; also the English frigate "Fury."

On the twenty-eighth, the Honorable Mr. Reed and his suite left the "Mississippi," and took up his quarters on board of the "Minnesota." The ensign was hauled down from our main, and Captain Nicholson's pennant ("coach-whip" the sailors call it) hoisted in its place. On the thirtieth, Mr. Reed made his first visit up the mouth of the Peiho, in the "Antelope," accompanied by his suite, Lieut. R. N. Stemble, Dr. John L. Fox, and Mr. Brown, captain's clerk. They took the little "Peiho" in tow. May second, blowing a gale from the north-east; let go port-bow anchor; heavy cannonading heard in the direction of the river. Third, the writer went up to the river with Capt. Nicholson and Mr. Reed, and others; found the "Antelope" had dragged on to the edge of the bank in the gale; had a fine view of the forts, and all the preparation for battle. The forts showed a strong defence; while the gun-boats in the river had all been put in a complete state for action, having their battle-nets up, &c. A perfect warlike appearance prevailed in all directions; while the Chinese were hard at work throwing up breastworks, placing their guns, and laying obstructions in the mouth of the river. Mr. Reed and his party proceeded to the beach, and were well received by the mandarins, who agreed to give the honorable gentleman an audience on the following day at sundown. Returned to the ship highly pleased with my second visit to the seat of war. Fourth, at daylight this morning, while I. A. F. Hulls, a private marine, was firing the daylight musket, it burst, tearing the piece all to atoms, injuring his hand very severely, and laying him up for several weeks.

Yesterday the Honorable Mr. Reed, his suite, and officers, were honored with an audience on shore. At noon they proceeded to the beach; arriving there, they were met by the Chinese commissioners, and Chinese troops, with music, who escorted the distinguished party to a tent erected near the forts, on the right of the river. The American party consisted of Mr. Reed; his suite; Capt. S. F. Dupont; and Capt. Sterrett, of the marines; and Midshipman F. B. Blake, from the "Minnesota;" and Lieut. R. N. Stemble; Dr. John L. Fox; and Sailing-Master George Bacon; Mr. Brown, captain's clerk, of the " Mississippi;" and Mr. Bradley, American Consul at Ningpo; and two sergeants from the " Minnesota," who proceeded ahead of this party, bearing the American flag, which for the first time floated at the mouth of the Peiho, and within sixty miles of the capital (Pekin) of China. Arriving at the tent, Chinese troops were drawn up on each side of the entrance, without arms, as a guard of honor. There they were met by a high mandarin, and by him introduced to the commissioners appointed to meet the minister. Tables were laid, upon which refreshments, consisting of rice, sweet-meats, cakes, wine, and tea, were provided for the party. At the centre table, Mr. Reed was seated with the interpreter and the governor and commissioners on his right, and Captain Dupont, Lieutenant Stemble, and Surgeon Fox on his left; while the other members of the party were seated at side tables. In the rear of these tables were standing forty-one red and black ball mandarins, all neatly attired in their native costume of silks and other gaudy articles. The interview lasted for about two hours; the commissioners promising to do all they could to give Mr. Reed what he asked for. The party then left the tent under the same escort, and proceeded to their boats, and returned to the " Antelope." All the time this party was on shore, some of the guns, loaded, with matches lit, were turned upon the party; showing plainly that they felt jealous of all outsiders, — "barbarians," as they termed Europeans.

From that day until the tenth every thing was quiet and dull in the gulf. All hands had become homesick, sad, and gloomy, and sick at the sight of the surrounding ships-of-war and gun-boats. No mails; no fresh provisions. Weather, wet, cold, and disagreable. In fact, all hands snarling at each other. In the meantime, Mr. Reed had taken up his quarters on board of the " Minnesota;" and his party of United States officers returned to their various ships. On the tenth, he again, with his suite, went up the river ; but what was the result of that visit was not made known. An English steamer, the " Coromandel," with two gun-boats in tow, arrived. Next day received a mail from the United States. Fourteenth, received from the authorities of Peiho pigs, sheep, eggs, fruit, &c., which we paid them for. Fifteenth was devoted to target exercise with the guns. A target was placed at twelve hundred feet from the ship, which was pretty well used up. Hawks, and numerous kinds of beautiful birds, playing about the ship; lighting upon the decks, eating the crumbs thrown out to them. Some of them were of a most beautiful plumage, almost equal to the birds of paradise.

The nineteenth was an exciting day in the gulf, news having reached the different ministers that the court at Pekin would not make any terms of settlement of the pending difficulties. Accordingly the English and French decided to make an attack upon the forts at the mouth of the Peiho the next morning; and the river at once assumed a lively and warlike appearance. The transport steamers, and seven gun-boats, of the allies, steamed up after dinner. The topmasts of their ships and frigates were sent down, their spare anchors were let go, and every thing done to leave them

secure as possible during the absence of nearly all of their officers and crews.
This all done, the steamers and gun-boats went alongside of the different
vessels comprising the fleets, and took on board troops, artillerymen, sailors,
scaling-ladders, and field-pieces. They also took the various launches and
cutters, filled with armed men, in tow. As they left their respective ships,
they gave three loud and long cheers for the Queen of England and the
Emperor of France, which made the welkin ring. To some it was their
last cheering; for they now sleep in the hero's grave, near the field where
they fell defending the honor of their country. At sunset they had all
crossed the bar, and were safe inside of the river, anchoring at a good distance from the fort.

The twentieth day of May, 1858, will long be remembered by many of
us, especially those who took part in the doings of the day, and also by
those of us who had the good fortune, if it can be styled good fortune, to witness a battle. It was a fine morning. As the day broke forth, every thing
was on tip-toe in the gulf to ascertain what would be the result of the day's
doings between the contending parties. At daylight, all the boats of the
"Minnesota" and "Mississippi," loaded with officers and men, left those
ships, and proceeded to the scene of action. I had, by orders of Captain
Nicholson and Surgeon J. L. Fox, the good luck to be one of the party.
We arrived up to the steamer "Antelope," which, with the Russian steamer,
was anchored in a good position, so as to command a fine view of all the
proceedings. Both vessels were filled with officers and men, from the
decks to the cross-trees, all anxiously waiting for the expected attack. At
eight, A.M., smoke was seen issuing from the smoke-stacks of the various
steamers and gun-boats; and great commotion was apparent on board of
them. The launches and cutters had field-pieces put into them, with artillerymen, and then dropped astern of the steamers, in readiness to be towed
up to the scene of battle. The tri-union flag of the allies was hoisted on
board of the "Slaney," a gun-boat, on board of which were the English
and French admirals. At ten minutes past ten, A.M., the excitement was
at the highest pitch, as the dispatch-steamer "Cormorant," of two guns, was
seen to move, and proceed up toward the forts. As she neared the fort on
the right, the Chinese commenced the battle by opening fire upon her: the
steamer kept on until within three hundred yards of the fort, when she returned the fire from her long forty-two; the shell taking effect in the fort.
The other gun-boats and steamers kept on after her; and the fight at half-
past ten was at its height. All five of the forts were throwing their shots in
every direction; while the allies were sending their shell, grape, and can-
nister into the forts at a terrible rate; and each shell told its work of destruction. The walls of the various forts began to yield to the terrible bat-
tering they had received from the allies. The gaudy flags had all been
levelled. The water batteries were now silenced. After the action began,
several of the shot fell within a few yards of the "Antelope;" but so excited
were we all that we heeded them not. It was an awful yet grand sight to

look at, — to see the shot and shell repassing each other, whistling through the air, and, as they fell, sending up rocks and earth heavenward. At this time the gun-boat "Slaney," with Admiral Sir Michael Seymour, of the English fleet, and Admiral R. de Genouilly, of the French fleet, on board, followed up after the other boats, taking in tow about twenty boats belonging to the various ships, all filled with marines, sailors, and artillerymen (which were selected as the different land parties). As she approached the forts she opened her fire upon them right and left, which they returned, striking her with their shots three or four times in the hull: her union union flag was shot partially away. One of the boats which she had in tow was pierced by an eighteen-pounder shot, killing several of the men in the same, and wounding several others. The boat was so shattered that she soon filled ; and the survivors made for the other boats, and a raft for landing purposes, which they had in tow. The wrecked boat floated down by the " Antelope," and was picked up by a boat's crew of the "Mississippi," and handed over to the officer in charge of the hospital-ship lying near us.

The " Cormorant," " Nimrod," and " Slaney," proceeded on up to the narrow mouth of the river; fighting their way through all five of the forts to the beach above them where the landing was effected under the cover of the guns. The French were first to land, which they done to the right of the river; while the English landed on the left. In landing, several were killed, and others wounded. As soon as they landed, they hurried up to the forts, which was the signal for a general stampede with the Chinese, who fled in every direction at the approach of the allies, leaving their forts and batteries to take care of themselves. They were soon in possession of the allies. The remaining flags were torn down, and the forts were in possession of the allies; their flags waving to the breeze from the same. When this was done the victorious party gave three hearty cheers; and then in good earnest they went to work to pull down and destroy what remained of the forts. Guns were capsized and spiked. It was a tremendous hard fight; and the Chinese, although beaten, fought to the last like heroes. By the watch, the battle occupied just one hour and thirty-five minutes, during which time over one hundred rounds were fired by the contending parties. The Chinese stood by their guns and fought manfully until the allies landed, when, like magic, they lost all hope, and fled in every direction, hotly pursued by the enraged allies, who shot the retreating Chinese like so many dogs. The officers in command were forced to step in front of their various commands to prevent their men from shooting down the poor devils as they deserted their guard.

Being in possession of the forts, the above-named boats kept on up the river (the rest having grounded) to three other forts above those taken, near the town of Tyn-sing. There another hot battle took place, which lasted for one hour, when the forts were deserted by the Chinese, and shortly afterwards blew up, with a most frightful explosion (they having been undermined by the Chinese before leaving), killing two of the French troops, and wounding several others, who were blown up high in the air, and badly burnt. A general engagement then took place in the streets and squares between the contending parties, the Chinese contesting every inch of ground. During this time, explosion after explosion took place in all parts of the town, sending up dense black smoke, rocks, earth, and other materials, to a fearful height in the air. It appeared that the streets, squares, &c., within half a dozen miles of Peiho, had been mined, before the attack, by the Chinese; and, when they found that they were defeated, the slow match was applied, and mine after mine blew up, presenting to every beholder a most frightful sight. Many lives were thus lost. The Chinese loss was very heavy; women and children, as well as men, were killed. In one of the forts, the Chinese women assisted to work the guns. The sight presented in the vicinity of the forts, after the battle was over, was most heart-rending: there lay the dead, the dying, and the wounded, calling in the most pitiful tones for help; but help was not to be had, for it was victory or death.

During the engagement, the first lieutenant of the French steamer "Fuse" was cut in two by a shot, killing him instantly. He was a brave and generous officer, loved by all who knew him. He was just giving orders to his men as he was shot dead. The sailing-master of the gun-boat "Opossum" was badly wounded; the carpenter of the "Calcutta" was instantly killed, while landing at the head of his men. In the afternoon, the wounded and killed were brought from the shore and gun-boats to the hospital-ship. One boat foundered, containing the body of the French lieutenant, covered over with the flag of his country, for which he laid down his life. Another boat was filled with poor fellows that had been blown up. Their clothes and the hair on their heads were all burnt off; and they were most shockingly burnt, presenting a fearful sight, and showing fully the effects of war.

Soon after the battle commenced, several junks were set on fire up the river, and cut adrift, by the Chinese, with the intention of making them come in contact with the gun-boats; but fortunately they grounded, and burnt to the water's edge without doing any damage. By three o'clock, P.M., all the forts were in possession of the allies, and what little of them remained was torn down by their men. It was admitted by all that the French fought the best, and ran the greatest risk in the heat of the battle. During the afternoon, one of the upper forts blew up, with a frightful explosion, scattering rocks, earth, &c., in all directions. It had been previously undermined; and, had it blown up fifteen minutes earlier, the result would have been shocking, as hundreds of the French troops had just left it a few minutes before it blew up. As it was, several of the English frigate "Pique's" men were badly wounded. The fighting on shore continued during the afternoon and evening; and mine after mine kept blowing up, presenting an awful sight,—the reports of which reminded me of the blowing up of powder-magazines, within the neighborhood of my own quiet country home. On the evening of the twenty-first, the gulf was illuminated by the burning of a number of junks, that had been set on fire by the allies.

The result of this battle was victorious, as everybody knows, to the allies, whose loss was fifteen killed and sixty-three wounded. The Chinese loss was very heavy. When the forts at the mouth of the river fell into the hands of the allies, one of the mandarins, who had been on board of our ship, before spoken of, to see Mr. Reed, committed suicide in the fort. He was found lying on his back, with his sword buried in his throat, grasped in both hands, and dead. He was in command of the troops in his fort (Philless), and, finding the same lost, he put an end to his life. When on board of our ship, he appeared to be a perfect Chinese gentleman, and was said to be an excellent man, and a scholar. But, by the laws of China, if an officer lose a battle with an enemy, he is sure to be beheaded, unless he takes his own life, which the poor fellow did, to please his young master, the Emperor of China. During all the night of the twenty-first, heavy cannonading was heard in the river.

On the afternoon of the twenty-second, we steamed up, and took on board the dispatches from the different squadrons, and left the gulf for Shanghae. At seven, A.M., on the twenty-sixth, we anchored, in a thick fog, in Woosung River. As the same began to break away, we discovered a side-wheel steamer on our port quarter, which was also at anchor; and she proved to be the U. S. Steam Frigate "Powhattan," Com. Josiah Tatnall's flag-ship. He at once ordered us to proceed to Hong Kong, fill up with coal and provisions, and proceed to Japan. Our mails, and some Chinese we brought down as passengers, were transferred to her, and two English officers (one bearer of dispatches to England) remained on board of us to go to Hong Kong. Accordingly, we left at two, P.M., through a new channel to us; but we soon had to break out of it, and take to the old passage, as we stuck in the mud, and could not get through the supposed new and short route. Twenty-seventh, passed an Ecuadorian barque; also made prisoners of some very large birds that chanced to venture on board of us. Anchored in the harbor of Hong Kong, at half-past seven, P. M., on Sunday, the thirtieth. Next morning, at eight, saluted the English Commodore, Elliott, with thirteen guns, which was returned from his ship. The first day of June we commenced to take in coal and provisions. Second, commenced to give liberty. On the eighth, James Grimes and Henry A. Ellsworth, two as worthless scamps as could be found, deserted. All hands were glad that they stepped out during our stop (of fifteen days). At this time the weather was extremely hot, sultry, and oppressive; so much so that it was deemed prudent not to allow the men to work during the middle of the day.

On the fifteenth of June, at three, P. M., we weighed the anchor, and left Hong Kong. Two days out, the diarrhœa showed itself in an epidemic form; ten and fifteen being attacked a day. When we arrived in that beautiful harbor, Nangasaki, we had forty-seven down with the disease. We arrived at the latter port on the twenty-third of the same month. As soon as we approached the shore, the signal-guns along the hills were fired, to announce to the people of the town that a stranger was approaching the harbor. Soon after we anchored, several high Japanese officials came off to the ship, accompanied by ten or fifteen lower-grade Japanese, — all of whom were armed with two swords, one long and one short one, — to ascertain who we were, and what was our wish. The chief spokesman spoke very good English, and was told by our first lieutenant that we came there as Americans, and that our visit was a friendly one. All this was put on paper by another *shinore*, who acted as a sort of clerk. With this he was very much pleased, and communicated the same to his comrades, who could not understand English. He said that he was happy to see us as such, and the governor at the same time would do all he could to make our visit a pleasant one. We had some officers sick, who wished to reside on shore for a few days, for the benefit of their health. Consent was at once obtained, and the sick officers immediately went on shore. Provisions were sent off to us at very reasonable prices. On the twenty-fourth, Captain Nicholson made his official visit to the governor. At the landing, he was met by several officials, who escorted him up to his excellency's residence. There he was most cordially received, and entertained with refreshments, &c. On the following day, the second governor of the island came off to the ship, in a barge most gaudily decorated with all kinds of flags and trimmings of Japanese artists, followed by large numbers of small junks and boats, well filled with the high and lower classes of officials, — all bearing those two swords, and neatly attired with the long silk gowns and breeches, with neat scarfs around their waists, and their hair neatly combed back, and secured on the top of their heads like a pig-tail. His excellency was received with fifteen guns, and the Japanese flag flying at our fore; while our excellent band performed some lively tunes, which appeared to please them very much. His suite and escort consisted of near one hundred. They were shown all over the ship, and they examined every part of her very closely; and, when they were shown into the engine-rooms, they appeared to be struck with amazement, — they were delighted with the engines, both of which shone like so much gold and silver. After inspecting every part of the ship, they were entertained with a collation in the cabin and ward-room. The twenty-ninth, it blew a strong gale of wind: no communication with the shore. Second of July, the second governor visited the ship again, with two high officials who wished to see the ship.

Sunday, the glorious Fourth, a day which every American — and every man that loves freedom — ought to love, was a cold and rainy day. Church-services were held on the quarter-deck. The fifth was also a wet and disagreeable day. At eight, A. M., we dressed ship with extra colors, and at noon fired a national salute of twenty-one guns, — which woke up all the Japanese, far and wide, whom we could distinctly see rushing down to the various hill-sides and landings, to see what Uncle Sam's boys were about, —

after which the band played our national air. The glory of firing the first national salute in honor of our independence, in the harbor of Nangasaki belongs to the good old "Mississippi." It was a dull anniversary to all on board. The weather was disagreeable, and no one had even thought of having a dance or an extra dinner ; and the day passed off, with the rain pouring down in torrents, accompanied by very sharp lightning, followed by frightful claps of thunder, that seemed as if they would sink all the surrounding beautiful hills and mountains.

On the tenth, early in the morning, the signal-guns at the outer station commenced firing, which were soon answered by those in the town, which gave us notice that a vessel was nigh. Shortly after, the frigate " Powhattan " hove in sight, from the gulf of Pecheli, — which gave us all joy, for she brought a tolerably good-sized letter-bag for the " Mississippi," the contents of which enlivened many a one's heart. Next day, the sick officers, three in number, came on board, much improved. Our sick-list had now swelled to fifty-eight, nearly all with diarrhœa and dysentery. On the fourteenth, the first governor paid his respects to the commodore. His barge, and eight or ten more boats that accompanied him off to the ship, were gaily dressed in all sorts of fanciful ways, accompanied with drums and fifes. Reaching the ship, he was honored with a salute of seventeen guns. He spent four hours on board of her ; and he and all of his numerous suite were richly entertained by Commodore Tatnall and Captain Pearson, two gentlemen who know how to do such things in a style that gains credit for themselves and the glorious country which they represent. From that ship he went on board of the " Mississippi," where he received another salute of seventeen guns, and, with his suite, was again put through a regular "course of sprouts" by Captain Nicholson, in the shape of the good things that are made for the inner man. They then inspected the ship, with which they seemed to be highly pleased, and then left her; each one, as he went over the side, bowing in the most polite manner to our captain, and all hands. Probably no nation can boast of so much *politeness* as the Japanese. They, in that respect, are a model for all the rest of the world, — at least as much of it as I have seen, and that is not a trifle. Seventeenth, a coal-heaver attached to the " Powhattan," who died suddenly, was buried. A Russian frigate, with Count Poutatain on board, arrived, when the usual salutes were exchanged.

It must be admitted by all who have had the good fortune to visit Nangasaki, that it is one of the most beautiful places in the world. The harbor is surrounded on all sides with hills and valleys, all beautifully filled with forest trees, and shrubbery of all kinds, of the richest varieties. Here and there are neat farm-houses built in the peculiar Japanese style, with well-cultivated farms, and some of the rarest and most charming birds of song sending forth their sweet notes. Every thing is delightful to the visitor. The town is laid out with wide streets, which are all gravelled, and neatly rolled. The buildings, which are generally not more than two stories high,

are mostly built of wood, and are divided into separate apartments by
sliding screens, which are made out of wood and fine white paper. In each
of these dwellings, the floor parts are covered over with a very heavy
thick matting, at least an inch thick, and are kept very neat. At the entrance
of all houses and shops, there is a small space or platform left uncovered,
where all who enter the same leave their shoes. You could not offer a
greater insult to them than to enter their houses with your shoes on. In
one room there is always a square space built of tile. In this, a charcoal
fire is constantly kept burning: over this, suspended from the ceiling
by means of a wire and hook, is the tea-kettle, so that hot water is at all
times at hand; and, as the Japanese are great tea-drinkers, the beverage
is readily prepared. They are great smokers, generally smoking a small
brass pipe, — holding about a half teaspoonfull of tobacco, of their own
raising, — with a stem from one to two feet in length. The temples in
the place, which are very numerous, are very extensive buildings, elegantly
ornamented with gildings, gold, and silver, with numerous idols in them.
They are open all the time; and enter one of them at any hour, and your
eyes would be sure to fall on some ignorant heathen, upon his bended knees,
offering up his devotions to the wooden gods. They perform them in the
most humble manner, bowing so low to the idols that they strike the
floor of the temple with their foreheads. Their devotions over, they rise
and proceed to a box, used for the purpose, and drop in a few pieces of
cash, and leave, — no doubt fully satisfied, that, as far as the soul is con-
cerned, they are safe. On the side of the hill, at the right of the town,
they have a very handsome burial-ground, surrounded on all sides with
trees, &c. Within this home of the dead, I saw some of the handsomest
monuments and gravestones that I have ever seen in any part of the world.
The bazaars are well filled with the rich laquered ware, and other fine
mechanical works, the production of this people.

The landing at Nangasaki, for foreigners, is at what is called the Dutch
Settlement, which is a small island, separated from Nangasaki proper by a
canal, which runs through the town, through which the surplus of rain in the
wet seasons passes. From this island, or Dutch town, you cross a well-built
bridge to enter Nangasaki. Before you cross the bridge you pass through
the custom-house, — a small building, with two apartments in it. There you
see three or four custom-house officials, sitting cross-legged on the mats,
eyeing all and every thing that passes from the Dutch town to the Japan side.
The Dutch settlement is under a commandant, and several officers, who are
regularly relieved, every three years. They carry on the lacquered ware
business, and they have also a factory for making machinery. The
Japanese can build a steam-engine equally as good as can be had in any
other part of the world. They are very ingenious. Let them look at any
kind of an article, and they at once have the idea how it is made, and will
go on and make a complete miniature of the article they have seen.
For instance, they built a beautiful model of the " Mississippi " out of glass,
which, in regard to the hull and spars, was almost exact.

The currency of Nangasaki is a paper currency, known as taéls, half, quarter, five hundreths, and one hundredths of the same. A taél is, of our currency, twenty cents. For a Mexican dollar they gave us five and a half taéls; so, by trading with them, we made ten cents on each dollar. During our stay in that port, two Japanese war-vessels laid near us. One was a fine-looking steamer, mounting four guns: her officers and men were all natives. Her officers visited the "Mississippi," and were delighted with her. The other one was a brig-rigged vessel, mounting two guns, — manned, as the steamer, with natives. During our stop in the port, three thousand Japanese, of all grades, visited the ship; all of them carrying their long and short swords, which are perfectly straight, and made of the finest steel, and so bright that they almost looked black. Every day, boat-loads of beautiful lacquered and bronze ware were brought on board for sale; and our officers and men embraced the opportunity to supply themselves with Japanese curiosities, to take home to their families and friends, as keepsakes from that wonderful country, which has been shut up from all the rest of the world, until America, with her fleet, and by kind words procured a part of her ports to be opened, — since which England, France, and Russia have done the same. But the glory of making the first step towards so great an object is due to the sons of Columbia.

Our visit to that port was the most pleasant one connected with the cruise. The governor, and other officials of the place, did all that was in their power to do to make our stay pleasant. Our officers, and such of the crew as had liberty to go on shore, were well treated, and received every attention from our new friends. Nangasaki will long be remembered by those who composed the ship's company of the "Mississippi," on her last cruise. When the death of Commodore Perry was communicated to them, they expressed deep regret. Although he did not visit that port, they had learned enough of him to form an attachment for him.

On the nineteenth, much against our own will, we left that port for Simoda, where we anchored in what is known as the lower harbor, at seven o'clock, P.M., on the twenty-third, nearly opposite the residence of Col. Harris, the American Consul-General, which is about one mile from Simoda proper. As we approached the harbor, running in among the sunken rocks and small islands, we discovered the stars and stripes floating to the breeze, surrounded by trees of all kinds. This was in the yard of the colonel's residence, which is in what was formerly occupied for a Buddha temple, which was given up by the Japanese government for the consul's residence. The consul's household consisted, besides himself, of an inter-preter (a Dutchman by birth), and three or four Chinese servants. From his office windows, he has for amusement, if it can be termed such, a very ancient graveyard to look at. In his front yard are several granite idols, protected from the weather with small roofs built over them, besides the orange, sago, and other trees. Over the main entrance to this temple is the American coat of arms.

Col. Harris is the first one that ever hoisted the consul's flag in Japan. He is from New York, and is every inch a gentleman; and he is highly thought of and beloved by the natives. Since he has been here he has done a great deal for our country; having secured a new treaty for our government, opening another and better port to us, — that of Kauagowa, near to the city of Jeddo. He deserves well of his country. Shortly after we anchored (by the way, I should mention that we were taken into port by a Japanese pilot, who came off to meet us in his boat, with the American flag flying at its stern, with which he seemed highly pleased), Mr. Harris came off to the ship; and for the first time for six months he received intelligence from his friends, or the government at home. We carried him a large mail, besides dispatches, &c. The old man was heartily glad to see us there, as he had, he said, almost thought that government had forgotten him. He bade Captain Nicholson and all the officers make his house their home; and in fact the latch-string of his house was out on the right side of the door. The consul is as gray as he can well be ; but he looked the picture of health and happiness, and moved round like a young man of twenty.

We anchored nearly in the same spot where the Russian ship-of-war, "Diana" was lost, a few years ago, during an earthquake. On the twenty-fifth, the frigate "Powhattan" came in. The little village in which Consul Harris resides is known as Suraki, a small fishing town, of about fifty houses. Immediately in the rear, and hanging over the town, is an immense mountain, at least a mile high, which is completely covered over with trees and shrubbery. It is grand to look at, beyond description.

Simoda is not so good-looking a place as Nangasaki. The streets are narrow, and at their intersections have gates, which can be easily closed, should any emergency require it. At various points are placed stone monuments, on which are inscribed the municipal laws of the place, so that the population can at all times be acquainted with the laws by which they are governed. The houses, which are all finished in an ornamental style of stucco-work, and other materials, are nearly all of one story, and without chimneys. On the roofs are various kinds of wire-work, ingeniously placed, so as to prevent the crows, which are very numerous in the town, from alighting on the same. Behind the town is a beautiful valley, which extends several miles, through which a plentiful stream of water flows. On the banks of this river are located rice and grain mills. The high and mountainous hills, which surround the town on all sides, are thickly wooded, and present a beautiful appearance from the shipping. There are about eighteen hundred houses in the town, each one of which contains from ten to fifteen inmates. The harbor of Simoda resembles very much in shape a fan. The town of Simoda is in a bight on the left of the harbor, and cannot be seen until you are well in, and pass the high bluffs which hide it from the entrance. Less than a mile from Simoda is a beautiful white, shiny beach, hard enough for a racecourse, over which the swell of the ocean sweeps twice a day. In the rear is a little village occupied by fish-

ermen. The people were extremely glad to see us, and were very polite and
civil. A comprador was furnished the ship, who supplied us with such
articles of provisions as we required. The town was free to all of us; and
every officer, man and boy, had the pleasure of going on shore to see the
wonders of Simoda. We met with no obstacles, neither was any one of us
followed by spies, as was the case on a former visit of the ship. On the
contrary, they would sing out to us as we passed, *Hi-o-you?* — in English,
"How do you do?" They tried to talk with us, so as to find out about our
ship, and our country. One intelligent-looking lad asked of me how far
America was, and how many days it would take to go there, which information was given to him. It made him look in wonderment to think the
ship had come almost twenty thousand miles to Japan. They would exa-
mine our clothes, and the quality of the cloth; pull open the seams, to see
how they were put together. The buttons on our clothes attracted their
attention very much, each one being anxious to procure one as a keepsake.
We wanted water : the day being very hot, and we being very thirsty, we
proceeded to a well to drink out of the bucket. A Japanese lass, of sixteen
summers, seeing this, she bade us desist. She then procured a pot, and
handed each one of our party a drink, which we kindly thanked her for,
bringing from her a bewitching smile.

The temples of Simoda, like those of Nangasaki, are commodious, and
well ornamented with any number of idols, and have plenty of worshippers.
These temples are situated in the most beautiful parts of the town, surrounded by all kinds of beautiful forest trees. Near to each temple are
curiously constructed bells of great weight and beauty, and of the best
musical sound ever heard. It is admitted by every one who has been to
Japan, that her bells are the best sounding ones in the world. In Simoda
are bath-houses, where male and female, the lady and the woman of the
town, gentlemen and loafers, all bathe together in a state of perfect nudity,
entirely unconcerned as to the moral effect of the same. These baths are
open to all, either to bathe, or to witness the sports of those bathing (if it
can be called sport). The bazaars of Simoda are more extensive, and are
filled with richer goods of lacquered, bronze, and porcelain ware, than
those at Nangasaki. In fact, the richest lacquered ware in the world can
only be found at Simoda. All bills that we contracted had to be paid at the
bazaars to a government officer. We had to pay in Mexican dollars: one
of our dollars, to pass for one hundred cents of our money, had to weigh
down three of the Japanese dollars.* In many cases our Mexican dollars
particularly those of 1856, would weigh down three and a half Japan dollars ;
consequently, we made sixteen and a-half cents on each dollar, as a Japan
dollar passes for thirty-three cents. It is a piece of silver one inch in length,
half an inch wide, and one-eighth of an inch thick ; with Japanese characters
stamped upon it. All who work for you, or of whom you purchase provisions

* Three " Itchobos. "

or other goods, have to be paid by that official, — you first paying him the hard dollars, and the official paying off the bills in their own currency. All the foreign money taken goes into the hands of the government, after which it is coined over into Japan currency.

In various niches, on the roadsides, and in almost every mountain, were to be seen idols of various sizes and descriptions, with a fresh bunch of flowers deposited near by. In the mariner's temple are to be seen, secured to some boards, the queues of Japanese seamen, who, during some storm, had been almost shipwrecked, together with a graphic account of the storm, in which they had so narrowly escaped total wreck.

The married women of Simoda, as well as of Nangasaki and Hakodadi, are known from the single ones by their teeth. As soon as a female is married, she paints her teeth black, and her lips of the reddest vermilion. The women of Japan are of low stature, and some of them are perfect beauties. In Japan, as in China, the females are thought little of by the other sex ; and they (or those of the poorer classes) perform a great deal of manual labor. The Japanese have the greatest hatred of the Chinese : they do not acknowledge them as neighbors, and were anxious to have us understand that they were not Chinese. At that port we took in ninety-six tons of coal, real Japanese stuff (who would have thought twenty years ago of an American man-of-war filling with coal at Japan ?); the labor being all done by Japanese, who receive the enormous sum of *ten cents* per day for their labor. These fellows, to the number of about fifty, were all in a state of nudity, with the exception of a cotton cloth around their loins, extending down to their knees.

On the twenty-seventh, the "Powhattan," with Consul Harris on board, sailed for Jeddo Bay, on official business. July 31, Alexander Doonan, a private marine, died at ten, P. M., from congestion of the brain. August 1, the commodore having returned from up the bay, divine services were held at the residence of Consul Harris. At nine, A. M., the boats of the "Powhattan" and the "Mississippi," containing Commodore Tatnall, Captains Nicholson, and Pearson, and nearly all the officers of both ships, and the Rev. Mr. Wood, the chaplain of the "Powhattan," with about three hundred men, left their respective ships, and proceeded to the shore. From thence they marched to the consul's house, where the reverend gentleman preached an excellent sermon. The house was surrounded by hundreds of Japanese, anxiously watching what was going on. Inside of the house were several (six) Christian Japanese, who had for some time been converted from heathenism. The services over, the party again returned to their ships, well pleased that they had once been permitted to worship God in that land of heathenism and idolatry. At half-past four, P. M., the boatswain and his mates sounded their pipes, and in a solemn manner called all hands to bury the dead. The coffin containing the deceased was placed on the quarter-deck, and covered over with the jack. All hands being mustered on the quarter-deck, the Rev. Mr. Wood, chaplain to the flag-ship, read the funeral services from the Episcopal Church form; after which the pall-bearers took the coffin and conveyed it over the gangway into the second cutter, the band playing the Dead March from "Saul;" and the band, marines, several petty officers, seamen, and several officers, got into the other boats; and the flags of the "Mississippi" and "Powhattan," as well as the flags of all the boats, being lowered to half-mast, the procession proceeded to the landing near the consul's residence. On reaching the shore, the funeral cortege was formed in the following order: Band; then James Pattison, Signal Quarter-Master, and an old veteran in the service, bearing the American flag shrouded in black; then came the military escort of thirty-six marines, followed by the coffin, supported by twelve pall-bearers; then came the petty officers, seamen, ordinary seamen, boys, and officers of the ship, — which then proceeded to the burial-ground, near the residence of the consul, the whole led by Lieutenant Jacob Reed, and the band playing the "Dead March." At the grave the address of the Rev. Mr. Wood was very affecting. The ceremony at the grave* being over, the procession was re-formed, and to the lively tune of "See the merry man returning from his grave," returned to their boats. Hundreds of Japanese followed the procession to the grave, anxious to see a Christian burial. The music, as the procession moved on in slow and solemn steps, appeared to attract their attention more than any thing else. The deceased was an Irishman by birth, but had been in the United States several years. He was a good soldier, and had served his adopted country as such for several years. A suitable gravestone was erected over him at the expense of his brother soldiers, who loved him in death as well as in life. He was a good man, and beloved by all his shipmates; and every thing that could be done to save his life was done by all connected with the medical department of the ship, but without avail. God had decreed that he must pay the great debt of nature, which he calmly did; and he now sleeps his final sleep in that far-distant country, Japan.

On the second, Surgeon J. L. Fox went on board the frigate "Powhattan," to proceed to Shanghae; and Surgeon William A. Spottswood, of that ship, joined the "Mississippi." The weather at Simoda was extremely hot and sultry. All hands were permitted to go on shore to scrub their hammocks and wash their clothes, and also to bathe in the surrounding rivers and brooks.

At six, A. M. on the third, hove up the anchor and left Simoda Harbor. I should add that we honored Consul Harris with an official salute of nine guns. On the fifth, stopped the engines about two hours to make some slight repairs. Whales, turtles, and porpoises were to be seen in all directions from the ship. At sunset, we were off the mouth of the Straits of Sanger. The afternoon of the sixth found us at anchor in the beautiful harbor of Hakodadi, after a pleasant run of three days. The weather being rather hazy, we did not have a view of the volcano Foogee. We found the

---

* Three volleys of muskets were fired.

current running with us at the rate of six knots per hour, which goes to prove the existence of a continuous current on the coast of Japan, similar in character and running in the same direction as the gulf-stream on our own coast. On entering the Straits of Sanger, we found the land quite remarkable, — that on the island of Yeso bold and sharply defined. In the vicinity, schools of whales were blowing in all directions. As we neared the straits, we found the temperature differing a good deal from that we had left at the two last ports; and all seemed delighted and improved by inhaling the beautiful breeze that swept over us. In a few days after our arrival at Hakodadi, our sick men began to recover fast.

The bay of Hakodadi is spacious and majestic in its sweep, and for facility of entrance and security for anchorage it cannot be surpassed by any other in any part of the world. For our purpose it is worth a hundred such narrow, contracted harbors as that of Simoda. It will make a grand and safe retreat for our whaleships — a number of which have already been there — to recruit and refit, procure wood, water, &c., and thereby avoid the long run from those seas to the Sandwich Islands; and it will also make as good a coal depot as Nangasaki, especially for the line of steamers that ere long will ply between San Francisco and China. The view from the ship, as I glanced around, reminded me very much of the famous Gibralter rock and bay. The town contains between four and five thousand houses. The number of inhabitants on the island is estimated to be about twenty-five thousand. The most prominent objects of interest are the temples, — one or two of which are between two and three hundred feet square, — the roofs of which are covered over with tile. The streets are quite wide, and run parallel with the water : they are rolled with gravel, and are kept quite clean ; the cross streets being narrower, and closed with gateways of wood. The houses are all of wood, one and two stories high, and are closely packed together. They all bear the mark of having been built a great many years. A few of them are painted ; but they are not so good-looking as they are in Nangasaki, the ground floors being all occupied as stores or shops for business. The roofs are covered with clapboards of two or three inches in width, and are secured to their places by a large number of cobble-stones, some of which weigh fifteen or twenty pounds. These stones answer the purpose of nails, and to the stranger present quite a ridiculous sight. Around and on top of many of these houses are barrels and tubs of water, ready in case of fire. The citizens have several little engines of their own invention, which are stationary. The police or mandarins are very numerous ; turn which way you will you are sure to come in contact with them.

As the ship neared the town, we discovered the American Flag peeping above the numerous houses and trees, which proved to be on the premises of Mr. Rice, the American Consul, who is a genuine Down-Easter, hailing from away down in the State of Maine. His very aspect and size are sufficient to impress these half savages. He stands six feet six inches, and weighs over two hundred and twenty-five pounds, with handsome long black whiskers, and a sharp, keen eye. He possesses all the qualifications to enable him to discharge the duties of his office to the satisfaction of his government (although there were several complaints made against him to Captain Nicholson of foul dealings, &c., with our men; but, as I was unable to find proof of the charges, I have no doubt that many of them were groundless). On several occasions the governor of the place attempted to interfere with him, but he always got the worst of it. The then governor was reported as being a very arrogant and despotic sort of man; and, as you will see, he endeavored during our stay to make the fore part of our visit any thing but agreeable. Shortly after our arrival, our gentlemanly Captain Nicholson sent him his respects, and requested him to appoint a day to receive his visit. The governor feigned sickness, and would not fix on a day. After some consideration, however, he yielded, and politely received our captain, and during our sojourn showed all the attention due to his rank. He also endeavored to throw obstacles in the consul's way in regard to his supplying the ship with provisions, &c.; but our Down-East six and a-half footer soon brought him to terms. After that his excellency was quiet. It seemed, at the time of our visit to that place, that the office of governor was (and still is) a very lucrative one, and that there were several high officials hard at work to procure the removal of the then acting governor. They wished to have a certain prince appointed in his place. This accounted in a measure for his excellency being a little troublesome, as he had to move very carefully, lest he should have gone behind the treaty, and thus made himself liable to be censured by the court at Jeddo.

The governor's residence is in the centre of the city, on the top of the hill. There is nothing worthy of note about his house, which is a plain two-story building, located about two hundred feet from the road. It is approached by a wide gravelled walk, on each side of which are handsome banks covered over with green grass. In the rear of these are rows of pine, fir, and other kinds of forest trees; and near the gateway of this Japanese palace is a small guard-house. All the arms I could discover there were two old Dutch flint muskets, and a two-pounder iron cannon on a truck, the wheels of which were one foot in diameter. This terrible howitzer stood in the doorway, pointing towards the road, and was all that afforded protection to the palace of Hakodadi.

On the Sunday after our arrival, I made my second visit on shore, accompanied with some friends, and landed on some fine stone steps at the custom-house,—the very same steps, perhaps, which Golowin descended from during his captivity forty years ago, after having been confined in stocks and cages for three years. Here we were met by a large party of custom-house officials, who welcomed us with a very polite bow. Passing up the yard, and out of the custom-house gate, we were met by hundreds of Japanese, young and old, anxious to catch a glimpse of us. The alarm was soon spread that there were strangers in town,—not, however, by the people, but by the dogs, of which the town is full. They seemed to scent us out the moment we landed, and during our whole journey through the town followed us, and set up an awful barking. A Japanese who could talk good English told us that these dogs smelled a stranger out the moment he landed. They are of a breed half wolf and half bull-dog, and are worse-looking than the cayotes of California and Mexico. Notwithstanding the warm reception the dogs gave us, we kept on our course; the people running out of their houses to look at us, while many of them saluted us with a polite *Hi-o-you?* — in English, " How do you do ? " At some places where we stopped for sight-seeing, the children would take a look at us, and then yell and take to their heels. We were not watched nor followed by any spies, as on the former visit of the ship, but were permitted to go where we pleased,—to enter their various temples, first taking off our shoes, which is required of all who enter them. Most of these edifices are handsomely ornamented with gold, silver, &c., with any number of idols placed in different parts of the buildings. They appear to have plenty of worshippers ; for we found a multitude, young and old, loafing or worshipping inside and around them.

As a means of defence to the city and harbor, they have erected at the extreme right of the latter a stone fort, mounting fifty guns of small calibre; also two made of brass, fifteen feet in length, and of nine-inch bore, with locks similar to those used in our own navy. A pattern of these was given to them by the lamented Perry when he was there on the first visit of the " Mississippi." If it should be necessary to attack the place with a naval force, this battery would not prevent an entrance into the harbor, owing to the fact that the entrance is so wide that vessels could pass in without coming within range of the guns of the fort. The two brass guns are of a very handsome workmanship, and are kept very bright. This fort is garrisoned by a large number of troops, like Nangasaki and Simoda. The mandarins and policemen carry two swords, a long and a short one. Their dress is the same as that of their neighbors of the other islands.

As a general thing, the people are not so tidy or good-looking as those of the other ports; and they do not display the same intelligence and polite-ness as their brethren of the other places, neither do they show that disposi-tion to make free with strangers, which we met with at Nangasaki. This, however, is to be attributed to the fact that his excellency the governor has a pretty sharp look-out over them.

During our rambles, we had the gratification of seeing several *Kurels;* there were then a large number of them in the place. They are most cer-tainly the ugliest-looking men I ever beheld. They are of short stature, are rather stout, and have large noses and very long ears, with beards ex-tending down to the centre of their body. The sight of them would be enough to clear Broadway or Washington street at once, should one of them happen to pass through those well-known avenues of New York and Boston. The hair on their heads was gray; in fact, their hands and every part of them that we could see, were more or less covered with gray hair. The

Island of Yeso is their home, and they number about thirty thousand. They are reported to be about half savage, and will not allow foreigners to go among them. They are most certainly, as a species of the human race, a great curiosity.

All goods or provisions sold have to pass through the custom-house. For example, I went into a store and bought some smoked salmon, which amounted in price to forty cents. The storekeeper did not dare to touch my Mexican dollar, but took the fish, and begged me to follow him to the custom-house. Arriving there, after a journey of nearly half a mile, the officer of customs received my dollar, and gave me my change and fish, the trader receiving his pay from that officer, — that is, what was left after paying export duty on an old dried-up salmon, that from its looks was smoked years before our government thought of sending the gallant Commodore Perry out to that country. This is the way all trade with foreigners is conducted. Even a few string-beans, cucumbers, and radishes have to pay that duty, and be inspected by an officer, before leaving the shore.

We visited the bazaars, and could not discover any thing different from that which we saw at the other ports, although every thing was higher in price. I cannot conceive in what way Captain Foote, or any one else, can think these bazaars are of much value to us in the way of imports. They do not carry on any manufacturing industry, save the lacquered and porcelain ware; and one good-sized New York clipper-ship could carry in one load all that the three ports which we visited contained. A two-hundred ton brig would probably lay there a year before she could fill up with a freight. For a depot for our steamships, both naval and commercial, and whaleships, to recruit, they are no doubt valuable to our country. One great difficulty is that the Japanese do not want to purchase from us; all they crave is the money. They will sell all they have, but will not buy of foreigners.

Most of the land in and around the city is rocky and barren; but that which is used for cultivation is of an excellent soil and loam, and neatly cultivated. The Japanese manufacture their own flour out of rice and wheat, which, after being thoroughly ground, are mixed together. Bread of no kind is to be had at Hakodadi, at any price. Fowls could be purchased for fifteen cents each, and eggs for one cent each. The natives live on rice, string-beans, radishes, and fish, which they cook in various ways.

A Yankee physician had already stuck up his shingle near the residence of Consul Rice. From appearances, I was led to judge that his calls were not often, and far between, and that it did not require more than a second of time to make his charges for his morning calls. His name is Bates, a graduate of the New York Medical College; and I believe he is a native of good old Massachusetts, whose sons can be found in all parts of the globe. He is very much of a gentleman. And no doubt, after those people leave off some of their prejudices, he will have a good practice, and reap a rich reward for the privations he has to undergo. He is quite a young man, and enjoys excellent health in his new and far-distant home.

The morals of the people of the place, like Simoda, are in rather a low state, if one can be allowed to judge from the manner in which they enjoy the luxury of bathing. They have numerous bathing-houses, in which males and females, young and old, all bathe together in a state of perfect nudity, while crowds of admiring spectators stand around to witness the sport. Modesty seems to be an accomplishment that the ladies of Japan have not yet learned. Ladies of rank, and women of the lowest character, married and single, gentlemen and loafers, bathe together, apparently as unconcerned at the moral effect of the scene as if they were enjoying the sports of a pic-nic party. Houses of a certain character appeared to be a government monopoly; for those disposed to visit them had to procure a ticket backed by a custom-house official.

During the spring of 1848, over forty whaleships bearing the American flag put into that port, to recruit, and refit ship. By the way, Consul Rice had already held a consul's court under the treaty; and there were then confined in the cages two whalemen, who had been tried before the consul, convicted, and sentenced as follows: one, a native of Philadelphia, for stealing rum (saki), to one year's confinement at hard labor; the other, a native of New York city, named Waters, for assaulting a prostitute with a knife, to one and a half year's confinement and hard labor.

There are two or three distilleries in the city for the manufacture of saki, of which there are two kinds, — the strong and the sweet. We paid a visit to a foundry, where the Japanese cast their guns. Here we found two very large brass cannon, partly completed; they were of about eight-inch bore. The workmen were very civil to us, and showed us all the various tools, and endeavored as well as they could to make us understand how they used them. We next visited a curriers' establishment; and here we found them using the same kind of tools our own curriers use, and dressing the hides in precisely the same manner. Otter skins and other valuable furs are to be had, but are rather scarce.

In every little bay or nook, which indents that extensive harbor or bay, are located small towns and villages, which present a very pretty sight, and add much to the beauty of the scenery. Nearly all the junks in that extensive harbor had sails that were made out of duck, which is manufactured at Jeddo; and, in fineness of quality, it far exceeds our navy duck.

The island possesses gold, lead, and coal mines, which only require capital to be turned to account. Copper has also been discovered, and, to a small extent, the Japanese work the mines. Tea and rice appear to be the two most important articles raised in the island; probably for the simple reason, that, when a man marries a female, one of the vows he has to make is that he will take care of her for life, and that he will find her plenty of tea and rice.

The marriage ceremony is very simple. When a man makes up his mind to take a certain lady, he has to give notice to the governor; he then takes his intended to an official mandarin, who marries them. In his presence the woman is forced to pledge herself to obey and live virtuously towards her husband. This is not, however, required of the husband. Let him the next day seek the society of other females, — the law will not punish him. Should the wife, however, seek the company of other men, she is at once divorced from her husband, and otherwise punished. The crime of theft is severely punished : for the second offence, it is visited with death, no matter how small the amount taken.

Hakodadi, like all other parts of the world, has its street beggars. They present quite a singular appearance. They wear a very large rimmed hat, a frock, and white leggings, and carry in their hands a small bell, which they ring as they come in front of a house or shop. They then commence to murmur something, until the woman of the establishment comes out, and gives them a few pieces of coin, about the tenth part of a cent. They then repeat a blessing on the donor, and proceed on to the next house. In Japan, all charities are bestowed by the females ; the males never give any thing.

In Hakodadi, the same regret was expressed for the death of the lamented Perry as was evinced at Nangasaki and Simoda. The American people may feel proud to know that the name of Perry will long be remembered in Japan.

With all the ignorance and idolatry the people possess, they are not without schools. A gentleman informed me that the city is divided into school districts, which are supported by a tax amounting to about seventeen cents of our money on each family. By the municipal laws, the head of the family is held responsible, and liable to be punished, if he or she, as the case may be, neglects to send the children to school. I think this rule would work well in some of our own large cities. On the fourteenth and fifteenth of August, the annual celebration of the schools took place. On those days, the children, with their parents and friends, to the number of several thousand, — the children all richly attired in red and other colored silks, with banners with mottoes upon them, and several large images of men, women, beasts, horses, &c., and accompanied with drums and fifes, — marched through the various streets; the little children making the air ring with their voices, cheering, &c. In the evening, they again paraded the streets ; each one bearing a lantern, of a much handsomer model than those of the Chinese. These illuminated the city, which presented a beautiful sight to those on board of the shipping in the harbor.

During one of my visits, I visited the American burial-place. It is a neat little spot ; and, if our government would appropriate a few hundred dollars, it could be made into a very neat and appropriate cemetery. There are two graves within the enclosure, which, from their appearance, seem to have been covered over a long time. Evergreens, and flowers of various kinds, are growing over them. It being Sunday with us (the Japanese have no Sabbath), it was a fit day to visit such a sacred spot, to drop one tear for our departed countrymen there sleeping.

From there I proceeded to the temple, near the consul's residence. After witnessing the ceremony of worshipping an idol, I took a look into the small building in the yard which contains one of them. It is made of wood, and represents a man of a very large stature. He is seated in an elegant chair, which, as well as the image, is richly ornamented with gold and silver. In front of this stands a sort of a table, on which are vases of flowers and plants. The building is about fifteen feet square, well ornamented, and is approached by ten stone steps. After you ascend these steps, you step on to a platform. In front of you is a grated window, through which you look at this wooden god. Here all the worshippers repair, after the services are over in the temple; and, putting their two hands together in front of their breasts, they repeat over some few words in a loud tone. This done, they then drop into a small opening in the window some pieces of cash.

I noticed that all the females that did this carried in their hands a bunch of flowers. I watched them a moment, and saw that they went into the graveyard close by. Tempted by curiosity, I followed them. Arriving at this sacred spot, I witnessed a most affecting sight. My eyes rested upon hundreds of monuments of all sizes and descriptions. On or near every one was a bunch of fresh flowers, which had been deposited there that day by the living friends of the sleeping dead. There were forty or fifty women there, engaged in sweeping the dirt off the gravestones of their dear departed ones, while others were arriving with bunches of fresh flowers. I watched their movements; and, as they approached the graves of their dear ones, they knelt down in front of them. Then, clasping their hands together, and looking directly upon the monument or gravestone in front of them, they offered a prayer, in a loud voice, to their idols. They then took up the old plants and dirt, depositing a fresh bunch against the stones. After this, they bowed their heads nearly to the ground, then rose and left. I discovered one elderly woman, who was accompanied by a little child, performing the same solemn ceremony over a neat granite monument. I could not help watching her movements. Her eyes were fastened upon the low mound of earth for a few moments, when she uttered something, which, being in Japanese, I could not understand; while the little child stood behind her, too young to comprehend that its sister or brother was sleeping its long sleep so near to its little feet. It was an affecting scene, and carried me back to the tomb which contains two of my own dear little ones. After she had finished her devotions, I approached her, and, pointing to the child by her side, and then to the grave, remarked that the little piccaniny lay there (meaning her child). She at once understood me; and, with a most affectionate smile (which seemed to convey the happiness she felt that a foreigner had noticed her), she replied, " Yes ! " and, bowing to me very modestly, she took her little companion by the hand, and left the home of the dead. I was informed that this custom of visiting the graves of deceased friends, and performing devotions there, is followed up regu larly every year by the female relatives of deceased persons, until the very severe cold weather and the fall of snow prevent them.

The winters are pretty severe, and snow falls to a considerable depth, and lies on the hills and mountains surrounding the city until late in June or July. The summers are not excessively hot; the nights, at all times of the year, being cool enough to lie under a blanket. I was also informed that consumption is rarely known on the island.

To give you an idea of the severity of their laws, I will relate a circumstance that happened during one of my visits on shore. After having strolled pretty well over the place, I returned to the custom-house landing, to take the boat for the ship. Being too early for the same, I sat down to copy off a few notes. While thus engaged, a fine young lad, of about fifteen, stood close by, watching my movements. After I had finished my notes, he spoke to me in very good English, and made several inquiries respecting the ship and our country; in reply to which questions, I endeavored to give him all the information in my power, which appeared to please him very much. I threw away the useless piece of paper which I had been copying from, when he picked it up, and carefully rolled it up and put it into his pocket. Seeing this, I handed him a half of a lead pencil which I had been using, and which he had been eyeing longingly. At this moment, a mandarin, with two swords, stepped up, and would not allow him to take my small gift; remarking at the same time, that if the boy took it, he should arrest him. This is only one of the many instances of the severity of Japanese laws.

No one, except he has business, or is a public officer, is permitted to enter inside of the custom-house gate; and, whenever one of our boats reached the shore, hundreds of the people were to be seen outside of the gate, eagerly watching to get a look at us, as we landed. If Minister Reed or Lord Elgin had been landing, I doubt if they would have attracted a larger crowd together. If one of us happened to stop a few moments in one of the streets, or in one of the shops, we were at once surrounded by large numbers of Japanese, who closely examined the buttons on our clothes, and the figure of the eagle, which they seemed to admire very much. They also examined the quality of our blue clothes (for white was not wanted, if it *was* the month of August), and tried to pull open the seams, so as to understand how they were put together. Our boots, shoes, and caps also attracted their attention.

The shoes that the women of Japan wear are very odd, consisting of a piece of wood the length of the foot; on the top is a strap, which passes between the big toe and the next one, and then on to the ankle. On the bottom is secured at each end a piece of wood about two inches wide, which raises the women so much higher from the ground. Those worn by the males are made out of woven grass: they rest flat upon the ground, and are secured to the feet in the same manner as those of the women. They are called sandals.

A large majority of the poorer class of the males, during the summer months, go almost in a state of nudity; wearing nothing but a narrow strip of cloth about their loins. In the winter months, they protect themselves from the severity of the weather with thick, heavy stuffed deer and other skins.

The floors of the dwelling-houses, like those at Nangasaki and Simoda, are all covered with thick straw carpetings. There is not much furniture in them, excepting that which is absolutely required for cooking purposes; and, as rice constitutes their principal food, not many articles are used in that line. This carpeting answers for the bed and chairs; for the Japanese all set cross-legged on the floor, like the Asiatics. Our noble tars were allowed to go on shore on several occasions, and to remain all night; and, when they returned to the ship, they spoke well of the good treatment they received from the Japanese.

On the seventh, honored Consul Rice with an official salute of seven guns. On the twelfth, Captain Nicholson, accompanied by his aids, made his official visit to the governor, and was well received by that functionary. Sixteenth, the ship dropped down the harbor ten miles, to fire at a target, which was well cut up. Returned to the anchorage same day. Eighteenth, boat-racing, &c.

On the twenty-fifth, His Excellency Takanoutzi-Simotza-Kanokazmi, Prince of Simotza, Governor of Hakodadi, accompanied by his suite, and a large delegation of mandarins, and other Japanese, left the custom-house, in their barges, — all of which were most elegantly decorated with streamers of every variety, presenting quite a gaudy appearance, — and proceeded to our ship. As his excellency neared the ship, the Japanese flag was unfurled at our fore. As he came over the side, he was received by Captain Nicholson and his officers,— the marines drawn up in a line, and the band playing "Hail Columbia,"— with a salute of thirteen guns. The governor was richly attired in his native costume, made out of the richest silks and velvets. Immediately in his rear followed a Japanese bearer of the governor's swords, which were of the finest steel, and richly ornamented with gold, silver, diamonds, and pearls. The party numbered about two hundred, all bearing their two swords. They were all neatly, and many of them richly, attired. His excellency looked like a man of sixty; and, from his bloated appearance, one would be led to believe that he used *saki* pretty freely. They were shown all over the ship; and the governor (through his interpreter) expressed himself delighted with her neat appearance. So inquisitive were some of his party, that they overhauled all the berths and bedding, and tried very hard to look in all the private drawers and lockers. Having inspected the ship to their entire satisfaction, they partook of a splendid collation with the captain and officers; and they gave it as their decided opinion, that Uncle Sam's whiskey and good old Madeira wine were much better than Japan *saki*. Late in the afternoon they left, highly pleased, no doubt, with the warm reception they received from all on board of the good old "Mississippi."

About this time, Irish potatoes made their appearance in the market; and being pretty cheap, all hands had a pretty good "tuck out" on them, during the remainder of our stop. Several of our sick men declared that this God-send of Irish potatoes actually cured them of the diarrhœa. The way some of our shipmates stowed them into their inner man was a pretty certain evidence that they would either kill or cure; and, as we brought all hands from that port, suffice it to say, that *Irish potatoes, raised in Japan, cure the diarrhœa.*

On the second of September, our first launch, in charge of Master George Bacon, and crew, with Dr. Spottswood, and two or three other officers, in-cluding Assistant-Surgeon Wales, left the ship, on an exploring expedition around the bay. The morning was fine; but towards noon, the wind came out fresh from the south-east, and soon increased to a perfect gale, causing a heavy swell in the harbor, and making the hundreds of queer-looking junks there riding cut up all sorts of capers. The launch was over-taken in the gale, about ten miles from the ship. To return to the ship was impossible; and they decided to make a port in some lee nook, which they did. But they no sooner let go their anchor, than the heavy swell threw the launch and party high and dry upon the beach.

Here was a sad misfortune,— no over-coats, and the rain pouring down in torrents. Their allowance of grog being all played out, and night fast com-ing on, a consultation was held by the *shipwrecked mariners;* and, on motion of Surgeon Spottswood, it was decided to leave the *wreck,* and foot it up to the residence of Consul Rice,— a distance of ten miles, over a soft, sandy beach,—without coats, grog, or eatables. The line of march was taken up at dark, the launch being left to the care of herself. Surgeon Spottswood (who weighs over two hundred pounds) took the lead, slumping half-knee deep into the sand at every step, which made him puff and blow like a porpoise ; while the sweat poured from him as fast as the rain was descending upon him. With good fortitude, the party kept on without an interruption, save the barking and yells of the numerous dogs,— which, faithful to their masters, were only sounding the alarm that strangers were coming. The only luxury they had on their long and tiresome journey was half of a Spanish cigar, which was lighted at a "shanty," not far from the scene of the disaster; and each wrecked individual did his part, until the last of that cigar was smoked up. The party arrived at the consul's at half-past ten, P.M., completely wet through, and cold. Master Bacon and Surgeon Spotts-wood soon cheered up all hands, by ordering Fred, the consul's man, to bring out, not *saki,* but the best brandy and gin that the house afforded, which soon revived the shipwrecked mariners; and by ten, A.M., next day, they were safely landed on board the "Mississippi," in good condition.

When the gale subsided, a party was sent for the supposed wreck. They succeeded in returning her to the ship, in as good condition as when she left, without any loss to Uncle Sam.

Ninth, a party of officers proceeded on an excursion to the mines, in the interior. Twenty-fourth, James Lappan, a marine, was released, after being confined fifty-five days, for attempting to desert at Simoda.

For the last three weeks we have had a most splendid view of the comet. At times it was so bright that one could almost read from the light of its rays. Thirtieth, received the intelligence that the frigate "Powhattan" was at Nangasaki.

October first, preparing for sea; cornet hoisted to summon all hands on board of the ship. Second, at seven o'clock, A.M., left Hakodadi. Twenty-four on sick-list when we left that port. In the evening, the comet was unusually brilliant: the tail appeared to be of enormous length, branching out like a peacock's tail. Fourth, a fireman, named John Huttoon, badly cut in the face and arm, in a fracas with another fireman, named Francis Travis, who was confined in double irons, under the sentry's charge. At eleven, P.M., the martial music beats to call all hands to general quarters. The hammocks were all stowed, and the guns and every thing thereto connected were ready for action in six minutes. Late in the afternoon of the sixth, made land. Seventh, at seven, A.M., beat to quarters, and cleared the ship for action. (This was done on account of the news we received at Hakodadi, by the "New York Herald," that there probably would be a war between our country and England, growing out of the affair of the English cruisers in the gulf boarding our ships, &c.) The magazines were opened, all the guns loaded with powder and shell, and every thing ready to give our enemy a warm reception, — as we expected, that, if war was actually in force, some of John Bull's ugly-looking crafts might be lying at Nangasaki, waiting to catch us napping. But in that respect they would have been mistaken; for we smelled the rat, and did not intend to get bit by him, without showing a little fight.

At eight, A.M., off the entrance of the harbor of Nangasaki, the look-outs discover from the mast-head a sail. We make for her. She in turn stands for us. Great is the excitement. Just at this time, one old salt can see that she has got an English flag flying, while another offers to bet that she is a Russian. She nears us: the first lieutenant hails, "Stand to your quarters! silence fore and aft!" The old veteran of a signal quartermaster, James Pattison, whose locks tell that his share of time on this earth is nearly brought to a close, takes another look through his glass: he settles the war-question, for he declares her to be an American. All countenances now changed, — while the poor Englishman whom we shipped in Hong Kong, and who begged to be excused from fighting, because he felt too sick so to do, now begins to recover his health, and is the first man to jump on deck to catch a look at the approaching ship. (I mean John Ogilvia, an Englishman by birth, who ought to have been kicked out of the service at once.) We near each other; the signals are hoisted; and the strange craft proves to be the frigate "Minnesota," with the Honorable William B. Reed on board, from Nangasaki, bound to Shanghae. From her we learned that the expected war had all ended in smoke. The retreat is beat, — the magazines closed; and we proceeded up to the anchorage in Nangasaki, arriving there at eleven, A.M.

Here we found the frigate " Powhattan," which had a large letter-bag for us, and large quantities of the " New York Herald," and other papers, which were a God-send to us all, as we had not received any letters or papers from home for four months previous. Surgeon Fox returned to the " Mississippi," much to the joy of all hands; and Surgeon Spottswood returned to his ship, the " Powhattan."

Sunday, tenth, in the afternoon, divine service held on board of the ship; the Rev. Mr. Wood, of the flag-ship, officiating. During the services, the ship was shaken considerably by the effects of an earthquake; the weather at the time being very close and hot, and the heavens filled with heavy, dark clouds. The evening of the twelfth was the last seen of the comet.

Nineteenth, the Dutch commander gave a grand dinner-party on shore to Captain Nicholson and several of his officers, and Commodore Tatnall and his officers.

On the twenty-third, at daylight, left Nangasaki. At this time, our stay in that port was short; but the officials, and all others, showed us all the attention possible. It seemed as if they could not do enough to let us feel that they considered us as American friends. Our last visit, as well as the first, will long be remembered by the " Mississippi's " officers and men. *Nangasaki* will never be forgotten by them.

Twenty-sixth, at eleven, A.M., anchored off the town of Tin-Hae, eleven miles from Ningpo. Ship supplied with a small quantity of fresh provisions from a bumboat. Captain Nicholson made an official visit to the town, which is said to be the best-looking Chinese town, save Canton, on the coast of China. Its streets are rather wider than those of the other towns, with stores richly filled with the products of the country. It has " Josh-Houses " in every corner; and a public square, highly ornamented with images, Josh-paper, &c. The channel, from the sea up to the town, is full of Chinese pirates; and now and then an American, Englishman, and Frenchman is to be found among them. Mr. Bradley, the consul, being away on a visit, the Rev. Mr. Way, a missionary, was acting as consul. He, with his two interesting little daughters, visited the ship, and was honored with a salute of seven guns. He has been in the vicinity of Ningpo, in the capacity of missionary, for the last ten years; and his two daughters were born in the flowery kingdom (as it is sometimes called) of China. Before leaving there, we took on board John Riddell, *alias* John Odell, who had been detained as prisoner on the island of Chusan, on a charge of murder, for killing a Chinaman. When we arrived there, he was in the stocks; but the news of our arrival soon caused his release, and he was then turned over to the acting consul, who turned him over to us. We only had his story for the cause of his arrest; which, coming as it did, must be taken with a great deal of caution. He stated that he and three others were engaged in coasting from Ningpo among the numerous islands in that vicinity; that his vessel was boarded by a piratical craft; that he and his comrades, one of whom was killed, beat them off; in doing so, they killed four Chinamen; that for this they, the three remaining of his company, were captured, and confined in cages on that island, with chains around their necks, and an allowance of a pint of rice per day; that his comrades, all but himself, died of the cruelties received at the hands of the Chinese. How far this is true remains to be seen; for our captain did not consider his case one requiring much attention, and solely took him on board, and gave him a passage to Hong Kong. He hailed from Nantucket, and was not backward in boasting that money was to be made in China by pirating. It is to be doubted whether he did not merit the severe punishment he says he received while a prisoner on Chusan.

Thirtieth, at twelve, noon, steamed up, and left the channel, and proceeded towards Amoy, where we anchored at half-past four, P.M., on the second of November, in fifty-two and a half hours from port to port; the distance run being four hundred and eighty-seven miles, which may well be called smart sailing for the old "Mississippi;" being a little over nine knots per hour. It blowing very fresh, we anchored several miles outside of Amoy. Only one boat went up to the town. At five, A.M., on the third, steamed up, and left Amoy for Hong Kong; arriving there next day at half-past twelve, after a run of only thirty-seven and a half hours, where we found more letters and papers awaiting us. On the sixth, Admiral Sir Michael Seymour visited the ship, and was received with the usual salute. Eighth, commenced taking in coal, provisions, and water, to be in readiness for sea on the arrival of the commodore. Found none of the squadron in port.

Tenth, the weather very fine; but a scene was enacted in the harbor on that day that was painful to all who beheld it. It was the execution of a fellow-being for murder, — the particulars of which are these: A marine on board of the English war-steamer "Harper" had had a quarrel with the orderly sergeant: he ran below, procured a loaded musket, ran to the hatch, and fired at the sergeant, who was then ascending the ladder. The ball missed the object it was intended for, and took effect in the left breast of the second engineer, killing him instantly. For this, the offender was tried by a court-martial, convicted, and sentenced to be hung; which sentence was carried into effect on that day, at seven, A.M. The "Harper," with two other English steamers, and a gun-boat, proceeded to near the north entrance of the harbor; and there, in the presence of a large crowd of boats, containing Chinamen, sailors, and others, anxious to witness such a scene, the condemned culprit was, precisely at eight, A.M., swinging at the port fore yard-arm. He was dressed in sailors' clothes, and, after hanging one half hour, was taken down; and the steamers returned to their proper anchorage. In the afternoon, his body was buried at Happy Valley.

On the twelfth, the frigate "Powhattan" arrived from Shanghae. Nineteenth: commenced to give general liberty for forty-eight hours, and each man fifteen dollars in money. Eighteenth: a general court-martial convened on board of the ship, — Captain Samuel F. Dupont, president, — for the trial of several officers, and the fireman, for a felonious assault with intent to kill upon Huttoon. William Watson, a marine, returned from shore with his right collar-bone fractured. Twenty-fourth: medical survey held on sick men; seventeen condemned by the surveying board, and ordered to be sent home. Lt. W——, by the sentence of the court-martial, was put on furlough pay for one year, suspended for that time from duty, and dismissed from the squadron ; and he left the ship and went on board of the "Minnesota," to take passage for the United States, which ship arrived in port a few days after the arrival of the "Powhattan." Twenty-eighth : Lt. S—— went to duty to-day, the court having let him off with a slight reprimand. Twenty-ninth: at one o'clock, P.M., all hands were called to muster to hear the sentence of Francis Travis read, which was, that he was not guilty of the intent to kill, but that the court found him guilty of the assault, and sentenced him to be punished, by being confined thirty days in double irons, on bread and water, and to lose three months' pay, and be deprived of liberty for six months. Thirtieth : took in powder and sent seventeen sick men to the "Minnesota" for passage to the United States.

December fourth : the sentence of Joseph Perry, ordinary seaman, of the "Minnesota," tried and convicted of an assault upon one of the lieutenants of the "Powhattan," was read to all hands, — which was, that the said Perry be confined for thirty days in solitary confinement, on bread and water, forfeit four months' pay, be kept in confinement until the ship reaches the United States, and then to be dishonorably discharged from the service. Lieutenant Henry Esben left the ship on a sick ticket, and took passage in the overland-route steamer for home. Fifth : a large fire broke out in Hong Kong ; destroying several buildings, such as dwellings and stores, mostly occupied by Chinese. Sixth : wardroom officers give a grand dinner-party to several English and French officers, which Captain Nicholson attended.

Eighth : the "Minnesota," with the Hon. Mr. Reed on board, left for the United States, amid the cheers of all the squadron. The "Powhattan" gave her a salute, which the "Minnesota" returned. Then she saluted the minister with nineteen guns. The same mark of respect was shown to the distinguished gentleman by Admiral Seymour, and the French and Dutch ships-of-war, which were all returned by the "Minnesota." On the main truck of the latter ship, the "Minnesota," during all the firing, and as she left the harbor, a small boy was standing upright, waving in his hand the flag of his country. It was a beautiful sight, and added much to the scene.

On the tenth, at nine, A.M., left Hong Kong for Whampoa Reach ; anchored same afternoon near the Boco-Tigress Forts. Next day fired at targets placed on shore, which were completely cut up, showing pretty good proof that our sons of Neptune were fine marksmen. Same afternoon, went up to the reach. The " Powhattan " also arrived. Joseph D. Boss, wardroom cook, went on shore on liberty, at Hong Kong, and did not return to the ship. He was put down as a deserter, and his effects sold.

Lay here until the month of February, 1859; occupying our time in exercising, boat-racing, excursions, &c. Our men also got up a theatrical performance, which was carried out on two occasions in good style, to the entire satisfaction of all hands, and a large party of invited guest, — the crew having very generously contributed towards defraying the expense.

During our stay in the river, considerable excitement was created by the English and French attacking the ninety-six villages near to what is known as the White-Cloud Mountains, for a insult offered to General Van Straubenziae, the. commanding officer of the forces in Canton. During the engagement, two of the allies' gun-boats had their masts shot away, and another had her smoke-stack shot away. The battle lasted several hours, the Chinese fighting manfully. Finally the allies won the day, after having been repulsed three times. They destroyed several buildings, and killed a number of Chinese. Loss of the allies, six killed. They also made preparations to attack Fat-Chan, and mustered up all their gun-boats and troops from Hong Kong, and proceeded up to that place. Arriving there, they found all things quiet; were well received and feasted ; procured all the information they wished ; and then left without having the pleasure of firing a shot, or killing a Chinaman. Before we left the river, Lord Elgin came up, and also Admiral Seymour, both of whom we saluted with the usual salutes due their rank.

There has already been so much published about Canton, once the most famous city in the East, that I can hardly say more than that, at the first sight, one is struck with horror to look around outside as well as inside of the walls, and behold the destruction that the shell and shot of the enemy had caused.; also to see the once-noble factories of the European merchants all laid in ashes, having been set on fire and burnt by the Chinese. Within the walls, Yeh's palace (the monarch who for a few years reigned over that doomed city, and caused over seventy thousand of his subjects to be put to death) is all level with the ground. Not one stone is left where it was originally placed. After this villain was captured, over two millions of dollars in hard cash was found in a room in his palace; also the treaty which General Caleb Cushing made with this government a few years ago, which, it seems, had never reached the city of Pekin.

The temples inside of the city proper are tolerably well built buildings, and show that a large amount of money has been expended in their construction. They are well supplied with images. Josh-houses are as plenty as can well be conceived. The stores, such as were open during our sojourn in that vicinity, were well filled with all the rich products of the country. The city was then under strict martial law. To enter it, a pass had to be first obtained from the officer of the day ; then you had to procure the aid of a guide to show you the sights of the city. The Temple of

Horrors is a horrid-looking place : within its walls are to be seen images of the different modes of punishment — such as grinding to death, cutting in two, quartering, pouring hot lead down one's throat, sawing in two, disembowelling; and all kinds of machines for torturing a criminal to death. The Temple of Horan, on an island opposite the city, is where the disciples of Buddha worship him, — with his three faces, representing the past, present, and future. This building, with some out ones, covers a space of near forty acres, and an orange-garden, and a place for the burying of departed priests and men of wealth, twenty more acres. The building is surrounded by banyan trees. The main building is near two hundred feet square, and is filled with demons' images of wood, gilt, &c., intended to keep off the evil spirits ; together with about thirty gods of piety. Attached to this temple are over two hundred priests, all dining at the same time, and at the same table. Their food generally consists of rice and vegetables. They also have there their sacred pigs, as fat as they well can be made to be : they are never killed, but fed until they die with extra burden of fat. Nearly all this large number of priests smoke that deadly poison, opium, — the fumes of which can be smelled long before you enter the main entrance of the building. In Canton River, as well as at Hong Kong and Shanghae, there lie old hulks filled with opium, which is sold at an enormous profit to the Chinese, to smoke.

Whampoa is a small town, or collection of ugly-looking buildings, built over the muddy waters in the river, with only one principal narrow street running through it. Five minutes' walk, and the visitor sees all the sights to be seen in that Chinese town. Bartlett & Carey, two Americans, keep the only hotel, — that is, if a Chinese-built house can be called a hotel ; and for a glass of the very worst kind of liquor they charge the moderate price of twenty-five cents.

Bamboo, a town opposite, is if possible, a worse-looking place than Whampoa. Nentown is no better. They are three miserable, filthy-looking Chinese towns, with the stench of opium strong enough to knock one down. In the river are hundreds of boats, filled with men, women, and children, who have no other home, and who make a scanty subsistence by conveying people to and from the numerous ships always in the river ; while hundreds are almost starved to death, without clothing enough to protect their persons from the cold weather. During our stop in the river our extra food was daily distributed among the half-famished children that surrounded our ship. Christmas Day was celebrated by all hands; Old Sam, the well known bumboat-man, being engaged to supply all the messes with roast pigs, turkies, chickens, &c., which he did in good style. In the evening, the main-brace was spliced (that is, all hands treated to a tot of Uncle Sam's whiskey), by invitation of the captain; then old Schebel, with his band of all kinds of music, was got up, and all hands joined in the merry dance; some being dressed up in all sorts of rig, looking more like the Old One himself than any thing else.

The first of January, 1859, was duly celebrated with theatricals in the evening. The gentlemen who composed the company performed their parts well, and earned great credit for themselves, considering the bad state of the weather.

While in the river, our men enjoyed most excellent health; no accidents, no fighting, no punishments going on. All hands seemed to make our lonesome stop pass off as agreeably as possible.

Canton River, like all parts of China, is infested with Chinese pirates, who at times commit daring acts of piracy, mostly upon their own countrymen and their property. Their piratical junks are generally well armed, and manned by large crews of the most desperate villains in China.

On the seventh of February, we left Whampoa Reach, and the same afternoon came to anchor below the Boco-Tigress forts. Next morning had a target placed on shore, which was only four feet square. We then went to quarters, and fired three rounds of round shot; then a broadside of the same, — total, twenty-four shot, — twenty of which hit the target, or within three feet of it. We then fired three rounds of loaded shell at the spot where the target was first placed, which had been entirely cut to pieces by the previous firing. The discharge of shell was elegant, — better firing never was nor can be made than was done on that occasion. Had an enemy's ship been within our range, she would have been completely cut up. The distance from the ship to the target was seven hundred and fifty yards. This over, we exercised our field-pieces in the first and second launches, firing also at a target; which was well done. After this, we hove up anchor, and proceeded on our way to Hong Kong, where we arrived in the afternoon, and anchored near to the " Powhattan."

Next morning, U. S. Sloop " Germantown," from a cruise, arrived. During her absence, and while at Manilla, the cholera broke out on board of her, which proved fatal to two of her men. She also lost a lieutenant,— Charles W. Page, of Portsmouth, New Hampshire. He had his leg and ankle badly jammed by a gun's getting adrift. His leg was amputated; the result of which was his death in eight hours after the operation was performed.

We immediately commenced to take in coal, provisions, and water, to be in readiness for sea. We received orders from the commodore to be ready for sea in three days; and accordingly, Saturday afternoon, the twelfth, the ship was reported ready for sea. In the evening, our amateur club gave their last entertainment in China: the performances and scenery were well got up, and were admired by all hands, and a large party of invited guests.

Sunday, the next day, was spent in exchanging parting civilities with our friends on shore. Old Sam, the Chinese bumboat-man, flew around in all directions, collecting in his debts, which were all paid to him by the purser, amounting to nearly one thousand dollars. All debts due from the officers and men being paid up, we were ready for sea. In the evening the officers of the other ships of the squadron made us their farewell visit. At sunrise,

Monday morning, fourteenth, the cornet was hoisted at the fore to summons all hands on board ; and the smoke was to be seen escaping from over our smoke-stack. At ten, A. M., every thing being ready, all hands were called to heave up anchor, which call was quickly responded to by our gallant men. The anchor up, our black dogs of liberty let slip a salute of thirteen guns, — a parting salute with the commodore, — who gave us nine guns in return. Our band then struck up " Sweet Home," our noble ship moved on ; and by one, P. M., we were fairly out of sight of Hong Kong. By some mistake, no cheering took place, — each one waiting for the other to commence. We had been just thirteen months and two days on the station, the day we left it, and nineteen months in commission. Never was a ship's crew more rejoiced to leave a station than we were. Although a long route was before us, we were heartily glad to bid adieu to China. Two days out from Hong Kong, that loathsome disease, the small-pox, made its appearance. The infected individual was John Morris, landsman, whom we shipped two days before leaving that port. A temporary house was erected (out of canvas and spars) on the port-guard of the hurricane deck, in which he was placed, in charge of the surgeon's steward, and two men as nurses; and every other means adopted by Captain Nicholson, aided by Surgeon Fox, to prevent the disease from spreading amongst the ship's company.

Twentieth, had a strong north-east gale, which kicked up an ugly sea, causing the vessel to ship considerable water, and staving in the port-head. Twenty-second, spliced the main-brace in honor of the birthday of the illustrious Washington. Twenty-third, fine weather again. Twenty-sixth, we were again favored with a south-east gale ; which being favorable, we made considerable progress. The ship rolled badly.

We arrived in Simoda at six, P.M., on the twenty-seventh day of February, thirteen and a half days from Hong Kong, it having been the most boisterous passage made during the cruise. Soon after we anchored, the Japanese officials came on board, and welcomed us back to their port. Next day we learned that the English had been doing their best, while on a visit up the Bay of Jeddo, to induce the Japanese Government not to send an ambassador to the United States, until they were ready to send one to England. We found the American schooner " Wanderer," of Boston, in port, on a trading voyage with the Japanese. We also learned, that, during the past season, eight American vessels had visited the various ports, trading for lacquered ware.

Wishing to send Morris, the man sick with the small-pox, on shore, application was made to the authorities of the place by General Harris, to whose request they at once assented, and had a room put in comfortable order for his reception, in a building adjoining the Mariners' Temple, and then sent a large boat, and men, with several officials, to see that he was conveyed safely to his quarters,— which was done in the most comfortable manner possible. At the sick man's room every thing was furnished for his comfort ; two men from the ship having been detailed to remain with him as nurses, and Dr. Phillips remaining on shore as his attending physician. This was on the first of March. Same afternoon, General Townsend Harris, the American Consul, with baggage, came on board. At seven, A. M., on the second, we hove up our anchor, left Simoda, and proceeded up the Bay of Jeddo, and anchored off the town of Kanagarva. We immediately sent an officer on shore, to carry Captain Nicholson's and the consul's respects to the governor. Passing up the bay, we had a fine view of the burning volcano, Foogee Yama, and also of the building in which the late Commodore Perry made his treaty with the Japanese.

On the morning of the fourth, at ten A.M., His Highness Prince Na-Gwy-Gembano-Cami, governor of the place, accompanied by his suite and servants, came on board. As he came over the side of the ship, he was met by Captain Nicholson, Consul Harris, and the officers of the ship in full uniform, with the marines drawn up in a line presenting arms, and the band playing " Hail to the Chief." The imperial Japanese flag was hoisted at the fore, and saluted with seventeen guns. They were well entertained by Captain Nicholson and his officers, and shown over the ship, — with which they were highly pleased, and left in the afternoon well satisfied with their visit. Foogee Yama is over three thousand feet high, is nearly level on top, and covered over with snow. It is situated fifty miles in the interior; yet on clear days it can be distinctly seen from the shipping in the bay. The town of Kanagarva is a tolerably decent-looking place, but not so handsome or clean as Nangasaki. The streets are well laid out, and kept pretty clean ; and the stores and bazaars are constantly filled with the productions of the country. Temples are numerous, of large dimensions, and pretty well supplied with wooden gods, images, &c., which are all heavily and richly ornamented with gold, silver, and other costly articles. The temple " Diusee," a few miles from the town, is the largest in the country, and contains over one thousand images, wooden gods, &c. To this temple are attached over two hundred priests, who are supported by the money that is daily dropped into the cash-boxes at the temple, by the thousands who assemble there, to pay their devotions to the wooden gods.

We all had free use of the town ; and we were well treated by the inhabitants, who were very civil and polite. When any of us landed on the beach, we were surrounded by hundreds of those singular people, anxious to catch a glimpse of our white faces. During our stop in the bay, provisions were daily sent off from the shore, which were sold to us at very reasonable prices. For a Mexican dollar they allowed three of their's (itchobes), which are worth thirty-three cents each of our currency, and are of pure silver.

The Bay of Jeddo is capacious, and perfectly safe for a large fleet of shipping to ride at anchor at all times of the year. The weather is rather cold in the winter months, and considerable snow falls, and lies on the mountains in the interior until late in the summer.

The women of the place are very good-looking; and some of those we saw were very handsome. The married women are known from the single by having their teeth painted black, and their lips colored. The males wear the same kind of dress as their neighbors of the other islands. It consists of a loose sack; loose trousers secured at the knee; blue leggings; and grass shoes, or sandals, which are secured to the feet by means of a strap passing between the large toe and the next one to it. Around the waist they wear a scarf. On the back of their sacks is to be seen a star of different shapes and colors, denoting under what prince they serve. Their hair is nicely combed back, tied up in a queue, and secured to the top of the head. All the males, excepting the lower class, or rabble, wear two swords, — a long and short one ; some of which are very richly ornamented with diamonds, &c. The articles composing their dress are generally made from the richest satins and silks.

The laws of this place, like all the other towns, are very severe; and if, the unfortunate criminal happens to be a female, her chance of escaping punishment is very slim; for they rarely receive much mercy at the hands of the other sex, who should be their protectors. Theft, the second time, is punished with death, no matter how small the amount taken.

The population of Jeddo is reported to be not far from two millions. Kanagarva, Yokohama, Uraga, and all the adjacent country, are densely populated ; and the appearance of the inhabitants indicates that health prevails amongst them. *Saki* (rum) is their drink; but they seldom drink to excess, unless it is on some public day. Common schools are established, and the heads of all families are held responsible if their children do not attend. They are supported by a small tax levied upon the people. They are most certainly a happy people (that is, in their way of living), — more so, perhaps, than they will be ten years from now, when they will have had more intercourse with foreigners. They may yet curse the day that they opened their ports to " outside barbarians," as they and the Chinese have always regarded all foreigners.

It is very doubtful if they ever will consent to allow missionaries to reside among them in peace. The moment any foreigner attempts to promulgate a religion different from their own, difficulties will break out, that may be the cause of making it very unpleasant and unsafe for Europeans of any nation to remain among them. Idol-worship has been established ever since the country was first discovered, — how long before, no one can tell ; and to it they are so devotedly attached, that it will be a very hard matter to win them over to Christianity.

Near Yokohama, the building in which the first American treaty was formed with the Japanese was still standing unoccupied. During one of my rambles on shore at Kanagarva, I had a chance to see what homage the Japanese paid to the young members of the royal family. Myself and friend were leisurely walking along, viewing the many things to be seen, when suddenly we came to a cross street, where our attention was attracted by a large concourse of people. Prompted by curiosity, we stopped to see what was up, when we found that it was the procession conveying a young prince of fourteen years, on his way to pay a visit to some other member of the royal family. He was richly attired, in satins, silks, jewelry, &c. He was seated in a sedan-chair, borne by four servants. In his rear came his horse, led by a servant, which was most tastefully dressed with ribbons and other glittering articles. Then came his tutor; he was also seated on a sedan-chair, and borne by four servants. In his rear came his horse, led by a groom; then four other horses, all of which, as well as their leaders, were beautifully trimmed with all sorts of gay trimmings. As this novel procession moved on, the people all fell down upon their knees, and remained so until the royal gentleman had passed. We were requested to step one side; but we pretended not to understand the request, and therefore we had a good chance to look the young sprig of royalty in the face. He in return gave us also a pretty severe look, as much as to ask us what business we had to look at a Japanese prince. He leaned back in his chair with all the *sang froid* of a ruling monarch on his throne. Of all the people who knelt as he passed by, rich and poor, officers of state, &c., he appeared to take no notice.

Such is life in Japan. Those in power are very oppressive upon the people; and the strict laws of the country, which are very severe, keep the masses in a condition worse than that of the slaves of our own country.

Consul Harris having finished his official business, we left Kanagawa at three, A.M., on the twenty-first, and proceeded to Simoda; anchoring in that harbor at half-past twelve, same day. On the passage down, we passed within ten miles of the volcano Oho-Sima, and had a fine view of the same. It was vomiting up dense volumes of smoke and flames. It was a grand sight to look at. This volcano is held sacred by the Japanese, and by them worshipped. In port we found the schooner " Wanderer," having put back to that port badly injured in a gale of wind. Here we took in one hundred tons of Japan coal, which cost us only six dollars per ton, delivered in our bunkers; and the man Morris, whom we had left behind sick with the small-pox, fully recovered.

On the twenty-third, Captain Nicholson, and nearly all the officers in the ship, paid their respects to the governor at his palace on shore, where they were well entertained by his excellency. In the afternoon, in a fight on the orlop deck, John O'Brien, ordinary seaman, bit off a small portion of the ear of Stephen Dunnigan, a fireman. He was not blamed much for it; for the reason that Dunnigan, when O'Brien was drunk on shore at Hong Kong on liberty, had badly marked the said O'Brien. Dunnigan, therefore, received no more than his just reward for his cowardly attack upon a man under the influence of alcoholic drinks.

On the following day, His Excellency the Governor of Simoda, accompanied by a large suite, and several servants, visited the ship. They were received with all the honors due their rank, and a salute of thirteen guns; the Japanese flag flying at our fore. They inspected every part of the ship, and appeared to be perfectly at home.

Thirty-first of March, American bark "Morea," of New York, Captain Fletcher, from Hakodadi, arrived. From her we got a supply of Irish potatoes. Captain Fletcher stated that he was severely assaulted by Mr. Rice, the acting-consul at Hakodadi. Same day, the sloop-of-war, "Germantown," Commander Page, appeared off the harbor: sent all our boats to tow her in. Received letters and papers from her. She came up to stop us from going home by the way of the Pacific. She was too late, for that business had already been done. The ship had been on a reef near the Loo-Choo Islands, where she remained three hours. Shot and shell were thrown overboard to ease her, without effect; and she finally rolled herself off. Her rudder was badly injured.

The evening of the first of April, the "Mississippi's" dramatic company gave another theatrical performance, which was honored by the presence of Consul-General Harris, and secretary; Captain Fletcher and lady, of the American bark "Morea;" and several Japanese, who appeared to be delighted with the performances. The parts were well performed, and the company received the applause of all on board. On the evening of the fourth of April, our glee-club repaired on shore, and serenaded Consul Harris, who returned the compliment by inviting the club to partake of a collation, which was well got up for such short notice. On the sixth, at noon, the United States Ship "Germantown" sailed from Simoda, for Hong Kong, in order to proceed to Whampoa, to go into dock to overhaul her bottom, &c. We sent our letters by her, to convey the news that our intelligence of February last, informing them that we were homeward bound, was a little too fast; and to inform them that we were adrift, and it would be doubtful when we should reach home. Commenced getting ready for sea, — paying up bills. Japanese on board as thick as bees, evidently unwilling to have us leave them. The governor also came on board in the capacity of a common citizen; he, however, was soon espied out, and taken in charge by Captain Nicholson.

At four, P.M., sixth of April, the schooner "Wanderer's" repairs being all complete, sailed for Hong Kong. At six and a half, A.M., seventh, we left Simoda for Nangasaki, having on board Consul-General Harris; General Dorr, of Boston; and a Mr. Field, a merchant in some part of China, — as passengers. Mr. Harris accompanied us on the trip for the benefit of his health, which was somewhat impaired from his long residence in Simoda. It was a beautiful spring morning. The sun shone but with all its brilliancy; and under steam, and canvas (as the wind was dead aft), we soon lost sight of Simoda. During our stop of fifteen days in the port, we received every attention from the Japanese officials and others. In all their dealings with us they were polite, and perfectly honest; and I venture to affirm that they have the same to say of the "Mississippi" ship's company, who, on all occasions, on shipboard as well as on shore, had done all in their power to win the good opinions of their new Japanese friends. And I do not hesitate to say that not a word of complaint can be made by those wonderful people against officer or man attached to the good old " Mississippi," during her last visit to their country. In fact, I doubt not, if an inquiry should be instigated in all ports the ship has visited during the cruise, that the good people of those places would at once exclaim that the " Mississipi's " late officers and men were the best behaved that ever visited them.

Most certainly, our national seamen are rapidly improving. But a few years ago, when a ship-of-war arrived in our naval ports from a long cruise, the inhabitants always felt uneasy, for fear of the outbreak of these *wild man-of-war's men*, as they were then styled, who were then turned adrift. Extra police and watchmen were ordered out to preserve the peace; and 1 recollect, twenty or thirty years ago, when a ship-of-war's crew was paid off at Boston, what capers they would cut up, — pulling down houses, beating men and women, and committing all sorts of crimes. But what a change has taken place ! When a ship-of-war arrives in port, the people welcome the noble tars to their native land. No extra police or watchmen are needed; but the men receive their pay, and go to their families and friends. Frequently now their arrival in the United States is celebrated by processions, pic-nic parties, &c. May they continue to improve, until the navy shall be sought for by our young men from the back-woods, who are about trying their luck at sea, as well as the merchant service. This done, in a few years we shall find our navy composed of our own countrymen, and be proud to say that we at last have got a navy whose tars are " true-born Americans." This can be done, and will be done before many years; if not, the result will be that our ships-of-war will all be manned by foreign seamen. In making these remarks I intend not to cast any insult upon our foreign seamen; but they know as well as I do that it is a common remark, all over the world, that the American navy is composed of seamen from all nations; and English officers frequently take occasion to upbraid us with it. When they write home about any American ships-of-war, they are sure to say, amongst other things, that they saw on board of such a ship a number of fine English seamen. Therefore, in justice to our beloved country, if possible, let our ships-of-war be manned by our own sons of the back-woods and forests.

The second day out, we took strong gales from south-west, and from that the wind went all around the compass; and a very heavy, ugly cross-sea made our position any thing but agreeable. At times it was impossible to make any headway with a full force of steam on, so heavy was the sea. We shipped several seas, one of which made a flying visit into the wardroom through the skylight, after the officers had turned in, which created quite a commotion amongst the wardrobes, &c., of those officials. This weather lasted three days, when it cleared off, and the weather became very fine. In passing through the Vandiemen Straits we had a fine view of the volcano in full operation, on the island of that name. We passed within ten miles of it; and the sight was grand, as the black and white smoke towered aloft. The island is uninhabited, and is about two thousand feet high.

We arrived in Nangasaki at half-past four, P. M., on the 12th. There we found three American and ten or fifteen other vessels in port; presenting, probably for the first time, quite a business-like appearance in the harbor and town. We also learned that one of the bazaars had been burnt down, with all its valuable contents, during the past winter. The Russian frigate "Allscot," which we left in port the fall before, was undergoing repairs, having been very seriously injured in a typhoon, in September, 1858, on the coast of China, near Shanghæ. We also received the news that Consul-General Harris had been appointed Minister to Japan, which news was hailed with pleasure by all on board. A better man could not have been selected. President Buchanan did a good deed in nominating him; for he had worked hard for the interest of his country, and had done a large amount of good in Japan. The day following our arrival in the port, the Dutch resident minister visited Mr. Harris and Captain Nicholson, and was saluted with thirteen guns, and the Dutch flag hoisted at our fore, which salute was returned from the Dutch war-steamer "Balt," at anchor in the harbor.

One or two evenings afterwards, when the majority of all hands had retired to their quiet beds, or hammocks, the ship was all in commotion. It was soon ascertained to come from the birth-deck, where the orderly-serjeant, and duty-serjeant, F. Block, the exiled Pole, were hard at it, trying to black up each other's *handsome faces*. Blows were pretty freely passed, and bets ran high by the friends of the orderly that he would come off winner; but unfortunately his foot slipped down the hausehole, which suddenly put a stop to the fight. They were marched up to the mast, which resulted in an investigation; and the orderly was let off free, and poor Block was ordered to be confined as a prisoner under the sentry's charge, where he remained until the next day, when he was discharged, and told to "go and sin no more." The cause of the difficulty between the two distinguished military men was an insult offered to Block by the orderly, which he denied, and refused to apologize for. This is but a mere speck of the discipline of these fellows, and foreigners, that are put on board of our ships-of-war, as police and guard. Nine times out of ten this guard consists of the very worst of men, — the very rough and scourings of the lowest dens of our large cities. As I once heard the lamented and gallant Hull remark, "They are a useless piece of furniture, — on shipboard neither soldiers nor sailors; and only used, when in port, to be rigged up in an ugly-looking uniform, to make a great show to strangers, and to frighten away the loafers that generally hang around a ship-of-war in a foreign port, by pointing an unloaded musket at them." The sooner they are done away with, the sooner the navy will be improved by their absence.

One morning, while at Nangasaki, a good deal of excitement was created, from the fact becoming known that the midshipmen and assistant engineers had been indulging too freely, — not, however, in the "ardent," but in *mackerel*, which proved to be of the old Spanish kind. All the doctors, and their steward, with emetics, were called into requisition; and for about two hours; the steerages presented quite a ludicrous scene, — all hands sitting over slop-buckets, and heaving up the contents of their stomachs. This had the desired effect to relieve them of the poisonous food, and gave them such an appetite for their dinner, that, when they left the table their boys were forced to scrape the dishes pretty clean, and give the remaining chicken-bones an extra polish.

Previous to our departure, the governor and his suite, followed by a large crowd of Japanese, came on board to take his final leave of Consul Harris and Captain Nicholson; and he was honored with a salute of seventeen guns. Consul Walsh, the newly appointed consul to Nangasaki, and several other Americans, were among the invited guests. They were put through a regular course of sprouts by Captain Nicholson, in the shape of the good things, &c., including some good old Madeira, and whiskey. Next day Consul Walsh made his official visit to the ship, and was honored with a salute of seven guns. He had a formal and official introduction to the governor, at his residence.

Walter I. Clayton, a private marine, was confined under the sentry's charge for having ill-used a Japanese when he, Clayton, was on shore. A large number of the crew were permitted to go on shore on liberty.

Twenty-fifth April: John Davis, a seaman, met with a serious accident this afternoon by falling from the fore rigging, injuring his head, face, and wrists badly. His wounds were speedily attended to by the medical officers of the ship. We left the beautiful harbor of Nangasaki at half-past five, A. M., on the twenty-eighth of April, for Shanghae; taking a Russian officer of the frigate "Allscot," as passenger, and a letter-bag for the merchants and shipmasters of the various vessels we left in port. Same day spoke and boarded the American steamer "Yang-Tyee," bound to Nangasaki. Next day, "Wreck ho!" was hailed by the look-outs aloft. Bore down for the supposed wreck, which turned out to be a Chinese fishing junk at anchor, with all hands turned in below, and no one on deck to look out for any approaching danger.

We anchored in Woosung River at noon on the first of May. Next day, got under weigh; and, in proceeding down the river so as to turn round, we came in contact with a junk, carrying away our foreyard in the slings, and cutting the junk down to the water's edge on the starboard side with our wheel. In crossing the bar, we ran ashore in fifteen feet of water, owing to the ship's not minding her helm. We lay there for twelve hours, when we succeeded in hauling the ship off, and returned to the anchorage in Woosung River, much to the disappointment of all hands, who were in hopes that we should once see Shanghae during the cruise.

A few days ago, Sergeant Block, before spoken of, took a notion into his head to play the part of a lunatic by refusing duty, declaring that he would not do any more duty in the ship. For this high-handed offence, he was put under the sentry's charge, and placed in a straight-jacket. His insanity was undoubtedly a sham, got up for the very reason that he was too lazy to work, or keep himself and his clothes clean. He was one of Uncle Sam's hard bargains, and a nuisance to the navy and to himself. Report states that he has once been turned out of the army for worthlessness. He is one of the Polish humbugs.

During our stop at Woosung, the American ship "Vancouver," of Boston, was wrecked near an island called Gatsloff, fifty miles distant. One of her sick men was brought on board of us for medical treatment, he being very sick with fever. We sent a guard of marines, — ten men and two officers, all well armed, — to protect the property from pirates. They were absent from the ship three days, when the wreck was abandoned by her master.

On the twenty-seventh of May, the English Consul-General to Japan, Mr. Alcock, came on board of us, accompanied by several gentlemen, and presented to Mr. Harris the gold snuff-box sent to him by Queen Victoria. Short and happy speeches were made on the occasion. The box is about six inches in length by four wide, of pure gold; on the top the cyphers of the queen are encircled in a wreath of diamonds. The cost of the box is said to be about two thousand dollars. Mr. Erskine, the consul's interpreter, was also to receive a similar present.

Next day the frigate "Powhattan" got ashore on what is called the North Shore, about seven miles from the light-ship. We steamed up, as did the chartered steamer "Tay-Wan," and proceeded down to her relief; but before we reached her they had hauled her off without any damage, excepting the loss of an anchor and a few tons of coal, — thrown overboard to ease her. On returning to Woosung, in passing up the channel, which is at all times blocked up with ugly-looking junks, we came in contact with a Chinese pilot-boat, and snapped off her mast like a pipe-stem. Then we ran into an English ship, doing her considerable damage, carrying away our third cutter, and breaking her side in. The pilot came on board of us and wanted damages, but he was very politely shown by the corporal of the guard over the side. It was their own fault, for he had no right to anchor a ship in the place that he did. The captain of the Englishman also claimed damages: but our old war-hero gave him to understand, that, if he blocked up the highway, he must take the consequence; and off he went, swearing vengeance on all Yankee steamers of war, &c.

The commodore took up his quarters on board of this ship for a few days, and brought with him Mr. Consul-General Harris's commission as Minister to Japan.

On the second of June, took on board the band and marines of the "Powhattan," and several officers, and proceeded up to Shanghae at three P. M., to land them, with our marines, to form an escort for Minister Ward to visit the Chinese commissioners in the old city of Shanghae, to present his credentials to them. The procession was large, and was witnessed by at least fifty thousand people, mostly Chinamen. Arriving at the place of meet-

5

ing, the minister and his party were well received, and entertained with refreshments, also a salute from a four-pounder. In the evening, the party was entertained at the house of the wealthy Heards. Mr. Ward was the guest of the Heards during his stay in Shanghae. Next day he visited the English frigate "Cruiser," when he was received with a salute of fifteen guns, which we returned. Same day saluted the English Admiral Hope with thirteen guns, which was returned by the English frigate "Cruiser." General Ward and Rear-Admiral Sir James Hope visited the ship; and each of those distinguished gentlemen received the usual number of guns as a mark of respect due their respective ranks, with music and refreshments. Minister Harris also visited the admiral on board of his ship, and was honored with a salute of eleven guns, which we returned. General Ward and suite also visited him, and received fifteen guns, which we also returned. Nearly all the foreign consuls paid us a visit, and they were each honored with the usual salutes due their respective ranks. We were also visited by many of the foreign residents, including many ladies.

One night, before we left the port, half a dozen of our men concluded that they would take French liberty; so off they went. A part of them (three in number) came back in the morning, and were chained together hand and foot, and placed in the chain-locker, on bread and water, — which was paying very dear for their foolish conduct. A reward of twenty dollars for each of the others was handed to the police on shore, and they, two old hands, were brought back. Seven new hands that we shipped in Hong Kong we would not take back, — they being worthless.

On the afternoon of the fourteenth of June, William Wilson, a quarter-gunner, was so badly injured, while firing a salute on board of the frigate " Powhattan," that he lost his eyes; and his right arm had to be taken off at the shoulder-blade, which was successfully done by assistant-surgeon P. S. Wales of the " Mississippi."

Left Shanghae and Woosung on the fifteenth of June, for Japan, with Mr. Harris, the minister, on board; also E. M. Dorr, appointed consul to Kanagarva by Mr. Harris. On the sixteenth of June, Ferdinand Block (by birth a Pole) attempted to put an end to his existence by cutting his throat in a fit of insanity. He was prevented from accomplishing his purpose, and his wounds were sowed up by Dr. P. S. Wales. We arrived at Nangasaki at eight, A. M., on the eighteenth, three days from Shanghae, at which port five of our hands (whom we shipped in Hong Kong) deserted. A more worthless set of men never eat Uncle Sam's bread, and all hands were glad to get rid of them. Their names are as follows: John Anderson, Richard Lochlan, Albert Blackman, John Forrest, David Crossman.

At three, P.M., twenty-second day of June, steamed up and left Nangasaki for Simoda, where we arrived on the twenty-seventh, at 6, A.M., after a very rough passage of four and a half days. Found the American schooner "Wanderer" (King) in port, from Shanghae. Same day after our arrival, his excellency the governor, and his suite, visited the ship for the purpose of taking their last leave of the Hon. Mr. Harris and Captain Nicholson. The parting was very interesting. The governor expressed deep regret at losing Mr. Harris, and at having the port closed up. Next day, we struck Mr. Harris's flag, removed all of his effects on board of the "Wanderer;" and on the thirtieth we steamed up, took the "Wanderer" in tow, and proceeded up to the bay of Jeddo, where we anchored, after a run of nine hours. There we found that from fifty to seventy fine new buildings had been erected in Kanagaɪva and at Yokohama, such as dwellings and stores, in anticipation of the opening of the ports for trade, on the fourth of July. The Japanese were very glad to see us back again.

On the morning of the Fourth, at sunrise, we hoisted the American flag at each mast-head; and fired a salute of twenty-one guns, at noon, in honor of the glorious Anniversary of our Independence. At four, P.M., all hands were called to splice the main-brace, — that is, take a tot of whiskey free of cost. Same day, E. M. Dorr, the first consul to the port of Kanagarva from the United States, hoisted the American stars and stripes on his flag-staff in front of his residence in that port. The event was honored by an entertainment with the good things by the consul. Our Fourth was any thing but pleasant with us, from the fact, that, owing to the high price of the luxuries of the market, and the unsettled state of the currency, we were unable to procure any of the good things; and consequently we were forced to dine off old rusty pork and sour beans, with hard bread for dessert.

While we were in those ports, hundreds of boats hovered around the ship, loaded with men, women, and children, all anxious to get on board to see the ship, — a favor that was granted whenever the regular routine of the ship's duty would permit; and all those who came on board were greatly delighted with the sights to be seen on an American ship-of-war. Our engines and machinery attracted their attention more than any thing else; every part of which they examined very closely, and made inquiries respecting its use.

From Kanagarva we took a trip up to Sinnagarva, which is only six miles from the great city of Jeddo. Soon after our arrival, a junk came off with Japanese officials on board, to inform Mr. Harris that his house was ready for him. Found in port the English steamer " Sampson," and five Japanese war-vessels, two of which were propellers. Sinnagarva, like all the ports we visited in Japan, is composed of one-story buildings, closely packed together, each one containing a large number of inmates. They did not appear to be so intelligent and active a people as their neighbors at Nangasaki and Jeddo. The stores were well filled with all sorts of goods, &c. The married women there also paint their teeth black.

Jeddo is a large city, reported to be thirty-six miles in length, and half as wide; the streets and buildings resemble pretty much all the others. Like Sinnagarva, it has any quantity of temples and " Josh-Houses " for the worship of idols, &c. The temple or palace in which the emperor resides is a one-story, large, unpainted building, with nothing around it that can be termed very ornamental. The emperor has twelve wives and numerous children. He lives very sparingly : it is said that it does not cost over six hundred dollars per year to support his household. Near Jeddo, in the bay, and close in shore, are four forts, each mounted with about fifty guns, and manned by Japanese. Jeddo, or Yeddo, as it is termed by the Japanese, contains a population of over three millions. It is the largest city in the world. All of that large number resort to the various temples and " Josh-Houses " to pay their devotions to their wooden and stone gods, and other idols. As a large amount of valuable information has already been published to the world respecting Jeddo, it will be useless for me to dwell any longer upon that city or its wonderful people, who, it is to be hoped, will before many years see the error of their ways, and become good members of the great society of the world, and throw their idols to the dogs to play with.

On the fourth of July, the Dutch consul residing in Kanagarva visited the ship, and was saluted with seven guns. By the way, the Governor of Kannagarva gave up one of the small temples in that place to Mr. Dorr for his residence. On the seventh of July, at half-past nine, A.M., we manned our yards and fired a salute of seventeen guns; and, amid the cheers of the ship's company, the Hon. Townsend Harris, Minister to Japan, left the " Mississippi," accompanied by Captain Nicholson and several officers, all in full uniform, in five boats that had been provided by the order of the emperor, and proceeded to the landing in Jeddo. Arriving there, the party was met by a crowd of thousands of Japanese, who had collected there to witness the landing of a party of twenty-four Americans in that city, which to them was a novel and remarkable sight. The party all took seats in woramans (chairs), with the American flag carried at the head of the procession. It proceeded up to the temple Jan-Shooh-Jee, which had been appropriated to Mr. Harris, as the future residence of that distinguished gentleman. The streets through which the train passed were filled to suffocation with human beings, all crowding each other so as to obtain the best chance to catch a glimpse at us Americans on Jeddo soil. During our stop of two days, the official mandarins were in attendance upon us, and woramans were at our service (which we had to pay for). Under the escort of the officers, followed by a body of police to keep the crowd back, we were taken around the city to see the sights. At the temple, we were treated to a repast, got up in Japanese style. To each one of the party were two lacquered trays, each tray containing seven courses of refreshments; thus giving to every member of the party a taste of fourteen dishes of Japanese refreshments. That over, the party sat down to dinner with Mr. Harris; being the first party of foreigners that ever enjoyed that luxury, or had the privilege to stroll over the city, and to sleep within gunshot of the palace of the Emperor of Japan.

We found Jeddo to be much the best city or port that we had seen in Japan. Its temples are much larger, and the idols therein contained are much more expensive and very richly ornamented. The streets are wide and clean; the stores well filled with all kinds of goods, &c. The luxury of bathing is enjoyed in that city by the sexes together, perfectly unconcerned, as if it was all proper. The scenery in and around the adjoining country is delightful. The most prominent buildings are the ancient and modern *dimios*, which are generally occupied by the princes and merchants. They are very extensive, built on four sides, with yards and gardens in the centre. Within those palaces, the man can have as many wives as he may choose to select; and the first wife is the head of the family, and has to take charge of all the children that the whole family of wives may bear to their lord and master. The first wife paints her teeth black; but the others can do as they please, — paint or not.

The women of Jeddo are, as a general thing, very handsome, but they do not possess much modesty or decency; for they generally go with their shoulders, breast, and legs a long way above their knees, all uncovered. As it is the custom of their country so to go dressed, it is not considered by them as improper. The laboring class, or coolies, all go naked, only wearing a small sack around their loins.

The Japanese showed us every attention, as far as their orders and laws would permit; and in every respect they were perfectly civil and polite. The emperor's palace is in what is called the imperial district. It is divided into four classes: first, the emperor and his household; second, all the *hereditary princes;* third, the *ministers of state,* &c., &c., with their families, &c.; in the fourth all other officers of the government reside, and in this Mr. Harris resided when he made his first visit to Jeddo. Within that enclosure over one million of human beings reside, and all connected in some way with the offices of government; and no one outside of that district is permitted to enter the same without special permission. The town is protected by four forts, about two miles from the shore, mounting each ten small artillery pieces, which could be easily silenced in case of an attack by an enemy. Jeddo has her public schools, and all parents are, by an imperial law, compelled to send their children to the same.

Perhaps it will not come amiss here to give the names of the first American party that was permitted to enter Jeddo, to remain over night, and stroll through the city, — which, ever since it has been known, until 1859, had been closed against all outsiders. Here they are: Honorable Townsend Harris, Minister from the United States, to reside in that city; Captain W. C. Nicholson; Lieutenants Stemble, Pattison, and Reed (of the marines); Surgeon Spottswood; Chief Engineer Danby; Sailing-Master Bacon; Passed Assistant Surgeon Phillips; Assistant do. Wales; John Heard, Esq. (of China); Assistant Engineers Jackson and Williams; Midshipmen Pritchett, Kelly, and Yates; Third Assistant Engineer Desannor; Sailmaker Bradford; Carpenter Thompson; William F. Gragg, Surgeon's Steward; Samuel A. Stine, Armorer's Mate; Joseph Potter, Seaman; Thomas Seaman, and Theodore Husband, colored servants, and the first black men that ever stepped foot on Jeddo soil. The latter attracted great attention. The Japanese would go up to them, and rub their hands on their faces to see if the black would rub off; and when they found, to their surprise, that the color was fast, they stood and looked at them in amazement.

Our business being finished at the capital of Japan, we left that port on the twelfth, and proceeded to Kanagarva. Finding every thing right there with Mr. Dorr, our consul, we left that port on the thirteenth, and proceeded to Woosung. arriving there on the twenty-third. On the first of August, we proceeded up to Shanghae, by the request of the American consul and the American residents, to render them protection from the outbreak that was expected to take place amongst the Chinese, on account of the French barque "Gertrude" having, by her officers, been engaged in kidnapping coolies, to be conveyed out of the country, she then lying at Woosung. Some of the coolies attempted, on the night of the twenty-sixth of July, to leave the "Gertrude." In so doing, they were shot down, and several killed by the officers of the ship. This created a terrible excitement in Woosung and Shanghae, and the foreigners were in great fear of being injured by the enraged Chinese. We landed our marines, thirty-six guns, under Lieutenant Jacob. Reed, and one division of small arms of forty-eight guns, under the command of Lieutenant R. N. Stemble ; Midshipmen Kelly and Yates, and Passed Assistant Surgeon D. B. Phillips, and William F. Gragg, Surgeon's Steward. Two field-pieces were also sent on shore. After remaining fifty hours, the landing party was returned to the ship without being called into action. In going up to Shanghae, we ran into two ships, doing them a large amount of damage. We also ran ashore, where we lay forty-eight hours before we were able to haul off.

On the twelfth of August the cholera made its appearance on board. Next day we got under way, and dropped down to the anchorage at Woosung, when three more cases of cholera made their appearance. Every precaution was adopted by the captain, and officers connected with the medical department, to prevent the spreading of the fearful disease, which had the desired effect. None of the cases proved fatal. Our men liberally subscribed the sum of three hundred and seventy-five dollars for the relief of William Wilson, the quarter-gunner, that lost his arm and eye on board of the frigate "Powhattan." About this time the fever-and-ague made its appearance in the ship; and nearly every officer and man had a touch of the disagreeable disease. J. C. Hall, an ordinary seaman, was taken down with the cholera on the sixth of September, and died in nine hours, beloved and regretted by all.

On the eighth we left Woosung, taking the chartered steamer " Toeix-Wam" in tow, for Hong Kong; at which port we arrived on the thirteenth of September, after an absence of seven months, during which time we had been on constant duty, and the crew without liberty for ten months. When we left the river nearly all hands were afflicted with the fever-and-ague, and their emaciated forms showed plainly the effects of the climate upon them.

On the twenty-fifth, Midshipman Merchant, of the " Germantown," arrived in the mail steamer from Shanghae, bringing us our orders for home. This news created intense excitement on shipboard. Every one, officers as well as the men forward, were wild with joy ; and some dozen bottles of wine, &c., were used up on the occasion. On the following day commenced to get the ship in readiness for our long passage to our own native land. On the first of October, all things being ready, at half past six, A.M., we hove up our anchor, steamed up, and bid adieu to Hong Kong,—the band at the time playing " Sweet Home," and other national airs. The same day it became our painful duty to commit to the deep William Watson, a private marine, who died early that morning with dysentery. He was a good man and a faithful soldier.

We arrived at Singapore on the tenth, after a very rough and boisterous passage of nine and a half days. We saluted the town with twenty-one guns, which was returned from the fort. We also saluted Mr. Sullivan, the American consul, with nine guns. We there took in two hundred and fifty tons of coal, filled up with water, had a tuck-out on fresh provisions and fruit ; and at half-past five, on the morning of the fifteenth, we steamed up, and left Singapore, for Penang, where we arrived on the seventeenth. Before leaving Singapore, several Americans and others were entertained on shipboard with a feast of the good things, as a mark of parting friendship. In the Straits of Malacca, we passed the wreck of that ill fated ship, the " Sovereign of the Seas." Wreckers were alongside of her. We also passed a barque sunk, with nothing but her topmast out of water. She probably had struck on some one of the numerous and dangerous shoals and reefs in those straits, some of which we passed very near, and our wheels stirred up the mud on the bottom.

At Penang saluted the English flag with twenty-one guns, which was returned from the fort ; also saluted the American consul with nine guns. During our stop of four days at that port, we received every attention from the authorities, and European residents. Our band every afternoon went on shore, and performed for the amusement of the inhabitants ; and their sweet music was listened to by thousands of people. Our officers were entertained with a dinner-party by the English officers of the fort. Penang is a pretty place ; every house being nearly surrounded with cocoa-nut, and other kinds of trees. The land is low. It has its public schools, and nearly all the natives are pretty good scholars. Six miles ride out of town, over fine roads, brings you to the great waterfall in the high mountains back of the island, a view of which is grand beyond description. There are also to be seen acres of nutmeg fields, all in full growth.

On the twenty-second of October, we left Penang at eleven, A.M., for the Isle of France. At half-past eleven, A.M., on the twenty-third, John L. Schebel, master of the band, died of chronic dysentery. He retained his senses until the last moment, and made his will, — disposing of his property to his wife, children, and brothers, one of whom was on board of this ship as a member of the band. The next day, at nine, A.M., all hands were summoned by the boatswain and his mates, by the mournful sounds of their pipes, to bury the dead. The deceased was placed in the starboard gangway; and, his messmates forming around him, the funeral service was read by Captain Nicholson (the engines being stopped, and the flags hoisted at half-mast). At the words, " We commit this body to the deep," it was launched overboard by his messmates, there to rest until the great day when all men shall be summoned before the Great Judge. This being over, the boatswain pipes down, the bell rings, the engines move, the flags are hauled down, the ship moves rapidly from the lonely grave, and in a few days poor Schebel is hardly thought of. Such is life on board of a ship-of-war. One and another pass away on their long and last voyage; and in a few days they are entirely forgotten by all on board. The deceased was a good musician, and was a great favorite with the ship's company.

We arrived at Mauritius on the eighth of November, thirty-eight days from Hong Kong, which was considered a quick passage for the old " Mississippi." Eight of the days were spent in port. After we crossed the line, we had very fine weather; took the south-east trades. The ship's greatest run under steam alone was one hundred and seventy miles; under steam and canvas, two hundred and forty miles. On the passage from Hong Kong to Mauritius, we had a large sick list, mostly of fever-and-ague, — contracted while lying in Shanghae Harbor in August and September last. None of the cases proved fatal.

At Mauritius we hoisted the English flag, and saluted the town with twenty-one guns, which was returned from the fort on the hill in rear of the town ; also saluted the American consul with seven guns. The French consul received a salute of seven guns, when he came on board to pay his respects to Captain Nicholson. The ninth being the anniversary of the Prince of Wales, all the shipping in the harbor hoisted extra flags ; we also hoisted the English flag at our mainmast in honor of the *royal young gentleman*, and at noon fired a salute of twenty-one guns.

At half-past eight, A.M., on the fourteenth of November, we cast off our moorings and left Mauritius, having on board an English army officer, Major Scott, of Her Majesty's Ninth Regiment, who wished to take passage to Cape Town. Late in the afternoon of the same day, it turned out that we had another passenger on board who had not obtained permission to come. It was a black fellow, calling himself Harrison Sewall, a native of Boston. He belonged to an English ship laying in the latter port ; and, being badly used, he took that way of ridding himself of his cruel captain. He came on board of us the afternoon before ; and, aided no doubt by some of our colored men, he was secreted down amongst the rigging on the orlop-deck. His strange appearance amongst us created quite a stir for a few moments ; and, when taken aft before the captain, he could not refrain from laughing at the " black rascal," as he called him. An investigation took place ; and he, Sewall, was ordered to be washed, dressed in clean clothes, and provided with some food, which pleased him very much, as he had been fasting for the last twenty-four hours.

We arrived at Cape Town at ten, A.M., on the twenty-seventh day of November, after a passage of thirteen days from Mauritius. At six, P.M., on the twenty-second, the wind suddenly came out from the south-west, which soon increased to a hurricane, and continued to blow with great violence for seven hours: the wind, changing from all points of the compass, split the topsails, topgallantsails, &c. A very heavy sea was on at the time, and the rain falling in torrents. At one time it was feared that the spars would go over the sides, it being almost impossible to get the sails off her, which was done with great difficulty.

Passed only six different vessels on the passage from Penang to Cape Town. We passed from the Indian into the Atlantic Ocean late on the night of the twenty-seventh of November, fifty-eight days from Hong Kong; making the passage from that port to Cape Town in forty-five sailing days. We stood off that night, and ran into port early the next day. It being very thick and foggy, it was difficult to tell accurately our position. An Englishman spied us out, and came off, and offered to take us in for one hundred dollars. (There are no pilots at the cape.) He was mighty soon informed by the captain that his services were not wanted, and was very politely told to leave the ship in double-quick time for his impertinence. Our black passenger, Harrison Sewall, was sent on shore. As he deserted from an English ship, he was put ashore on English soil, although he claimed to be an American. The weather during our stop at the cape, part of the time, was very rough, which impeded our getting coal on board very much. A part of one lighter load was thrown over board; and another, containing a hundred and fifty bags of coal, sank alongside of the ship, — the lighter becoming a total loss to the unfortunate owner, who lost all the means he had of obtaining a livelihood. Hoisted the English flag at our fore, and saluted the town with twenty-one guns, which was returned from the water battery. Found provisions of all kinds very high. Saluted Consul Holmes with seven guns. At Cape Town, four men and one apprentice-boy deserted; and a more worthless set of men never disgraced a ship than those same fellows. The apprentice-boy had every chance to have done well, and to have made a good member of society; but his temper was beyond control, and for one so young he was badly addicted to intemperance whenever he had opportunity. The second day out from Cape Town, we discovered that we had another passenger on board, who had been, by the aid of some of the ship's company, secreted below. He hailed from Boston, and gave his name as John McCornoolon. He was severely reprimanded by the captain, and then sent into the coal-bunkers to work.

At half-past five, on the sixth of December, we steamed up and left Cape Town, and, as the sailors say, came rolling on home with a heavy rolling swell. Our last visit to Cape Town was a very pleasant one to all. At daylight on the tenth of December, in latitude 27° 12′ south, took off a

6

part of the buckets from the wheels, and put the ship under canvass alone; this being done in order to make our coal last us to reach St. Thomas. The wind at the time was very light from south-east, — weather delightful. Early on the morning of the fifteenth of December, a sail was made out ahead by the look-out aloft, hull down. At noon next day, we neared her, and she showed Dutch colors (barque-rigged). Same afternoon we passed her, and at night she was hull down astern of us. This may be considered a pretty fair beat for the old-fashioned side-wheel steamer "Mississippi;" considering that we used no steam, and had no extra quantity of canvas spread.

On the twenty-third of the same month, it became our painful duty to commit to the deep another of our shipmates, George Jennings, seaman, a native of Baltimore, who died early on that day with dysentery. He was aged forty-seven, and had been a long time in the service. At half-past three, P.M., the ship was hove to, the flag hoisted at half-mast, and all hands called to bury the dead. The deceased was placed on a plank in the port gangway, and the band played a dirge; after which the funeral service was read by Lieutenant R. N. Stemble, when the body was committed to the deep. The boatswain piped down; the band played a quick step; the yards were again braced to the wind; and the ship kept on her course, as unconcerned as if nothing of so solemn a nature had just taken place. In a few days poor Jennings was forgotten by all.

Christmas Day was spent rather dull, as we had nothing extra to eat. At four, P.M., all hands called to "splice the main-brace,"—a tot of whiskey. In the evening, a small set-to took place on the hurricane deck, between a midshipman and an assistant-engineer. For a few moments the bets ran high in favor of the engineer; but a well-directed blow from the "middy" brought him to the deck, when friends interfered, and separated the parties. On close examination, it was ascertained that no blood had been drawn; and the parties, by advice of their friends, retired to their respective hammocks, to reflect over the follies of living too fast on Christmas Day.

On the twenty-ninth of December, in latitude 3° 40' south, passed a French barque, close-hauled on the wind; making only the second vessel we had seen since leaving Cape Town, a distance of over three thousand miles. To pass away the time, general and division quarters, and field-piece exercise, were kept up almost daily, and with as much vigor as if the ship had been bound out to her station, instead of returning home. This was as it should be; as a large majority of the men will no doubt re-enter the service. They will therefore go on board of their new ship fully acquainted with all the various drills which are actually and highly necessary on board of a well-disciplined ship.

In regard to the crew of the "Mississippi," they may be set down as the best-drilled ship's company that has returned home for many years. And of our departed shipmates, who have died during the cruise, — and who are either buried in a foreign land or in the mighty deep, — let it be said, that, during their illness, their shipmates showed them all the attention that their various duties would permit.' Surgeon J. L. Fox, and Doctors Phillips and Wales, were untiring in their duties towards the afflicted, always ready to sit alongside of the cot of the sick, and in their kind and humane manner strive to make their sufferings as light as possible.

We crossed the line, in longitude 30° 4' west, on the night of the thirtieth of December. Next day, the wind left us; and, in lat. 1° 5' north, the buckets were replaced, and steam put on again. We made two thousand eight hundred and seventy miles, under canvass, in twenty-one days and twelve hours. We crossed the line with a seven-knot breeze, and delightful weather,—no rain or squalls. We had a most delightful passage from Hong Kong to the line, with the exception of a heavy blow, of six hours' duration, in the Indian Ocean. Perhaps it seldom falls to the lot of a ship to sail such a long distance without encountering some bad weather. Leave out that blow, and our launch would have lived in any part of the ocean we had thus far travelled. After putting steam on again, the ship was kept away for Barbadoes; at which port we arrived on the ninth day of January, after a most remarkably pleasant passage of thirty-four days, from Cape Town. There we sent a boat in to ascertain if we could get coal. The result was we could not; and we left again on the same day, and arrived at Saint Thomas on the twelfth of the same month. There we saluted the Danish flag with twenty-one guns, which was returned from the fort; also honored the American consul with a salute of seven guns, when he came on board of the ship. Took on board coal, wood, and water, and left again on the seventeenth. Before our leaving, Consul Warring gave a grand dinner-party to Captain Nicholson and officers. He also, accompanied by his family, and a large party of gentlemen and ladies, attended church services on board of us; and they were entertained with a sumptuous repast by the ward-room officers. Amongst them was Gen. Soto, with his lady and son. The general was, and still remains, the warm and near friend of General Santa Anna, and is now residing in exile with him. The general expressed, in warm terms, his thanks for the flattering reception he received on board of us, and expressed his wish that at no distant day he should see his unfortunate country under American rule, with the stars and stripes waving in every city and town.

We lost our port-bow anchor, and fifteen fathoms of chain, in that port. The divers could not find it; so we steamed up, and left it to rest in its dark bed. We arrived in Boston Harbor on the twenty-seventh of January, having made one of the most remarkable passages home from China that ever was made; not being in any heavy gales or squalls, worthy of note, until we arrived off Boston Bay, on the twenty-fifth of January. Here we took a heavy north-wester; during which, to our sad disappointment, our starboard engine became useless, by the breaking of the cross-tail. It took all the next day to patch it up, in order to reach our port in safety; but it was of no use to us. We reached our port with the port engine, and the aid of canvas.

In conclusion, I can say that our cruise of thirty-one months in China permitted to go on shore in the latter country, they have th.s had t privilege of seeing and learning much of that wonderful country and people. In China, our duties were arduous: but all duties were promp performed with credit to us all, and to the honor of our glorious countr and, as a general thing, I feel confidant that all hands will look back w pleasure to their late cruise in the "Mississippi." To be sure, there have be many ups and downs, and our hardships in many instances have be trying; but in all cases it has, I think, been the aim of every man to do best to make the cruise pleasant. And, in regard to Captain William Nicholson and his officers, I think every one will admit the fact that th have extended good treatment towards all hands, and every favor tl could have reasonably been expected. Few ships leave the United Sta whose crews are allowed more liberty than was granted to our shi company; and it seldom occurs that so much money is served out durin; cruise as has been served on board of the good old "Mississippi." At finally, it will be admitted that our cruise has been as pleasant as could p sibly have been expected in such a miserable country as China; and hands, in after-years, will look back upon Captain William C. Nicholson a true sailors' friend.

The ship has run a little over forty-seven thousand miles. There ha been fired during the cruise sixty-five salutes, in all nine hundred and six nine guns; besides nearly one thousand guns fired at targets and for otl purposes. There has been burned on board of her seven thousand fi hundred and fifty tons of coal, costing not far from one hundred and twel thousand dollars. Four hundred and eighty thousand gallons of fresh wa has been used by the ship's company. Among the heavy articles of pi visions consumed during the cruise are seven hundred and eighty barr salt beef, five hundred and eighty-five barrels of salt pork, one hundi and fifty-five barrels of rice, one hundred and thirty barrels of beans, t hundred and eight thousand pounds of bread, seven thousand one hundi and eighty pounds of butter; besides a vast amount of tea, sugar, pickl flour, vinegar, molasses, and thousands of pounds of fresh beef and veg tables. And no ship ever returned from China with her crew in beti health, or can boast of being called upon only seven times during t cruise to pay the last solemn mark of respect to departed shipmates. Wh she arrived, there was not an invalid amongst the men.

God grant, shipmates, that the remaining cruises that you make n be equally as fortunate! and, when this feeble hand shall be still in dea may you still be faithfully serving your country, with credit to yourselv and with honor to those glorious stars and stripes that have so often wav above your heads in every clime, even in far-distant Japan, — in whi beautiful and wonderful country you can all boast, and feel proud tell to others, that you have trodden upon the soil! Farewell, farewi shipmates!